PUB WALK[S]

IN

The Surrey Hills

Other areas covered in the Pub Walks series include:

Bedfordshire
Berkshire
Bristol and Bath
Buckinghamshire
Cheshire
The Chilterns
The Cotswolds
Dartmoor and South Devon
Derbyshire
Essex
Gloucestershire
Herefordshire
Hertfordshire
The Isle of Wight
Lancashire
Leicestershire and Rutland
Lincolnshire
Middlesex and West London
Norfolk
Northamptonshire
North Wales
Nottinghamshire
Oxfordshire
Shropshire
South Wales
Suffolk
Surrey
The Thames Valley
Warwickshire
Wiltshire
Worcestershire
East Yorkshire
North Yorkshire
South Yorkshire
West Yorkshire

A complete catalogue is available from the publisher at
3 Catherine Road, Newbury, Berkshire.

PUB WALKS IN The Surrey Hills

THIRTY CIRCULAR WALKS
AROUND INNS IN
THE SURREY HILLS

Derek Palmer

COUNTRYSIDE BOOKS
NEWBURY, BERKSHIRE

First Published 1994

COUNTRYSIDE BOOKS
3 Catherine Road
Newbury, Berkshire

ISBN 1 85306 308 8

Designed by Mon Mohan
Cover illustration by Colin Doggett
Photographs by the author
Maps by Brenda Palmer

Produced through MRM Associates Ltd., Reading
Typeset by Paragon Typesetters, Queensferry, Clwyd
Printed in England

Contents

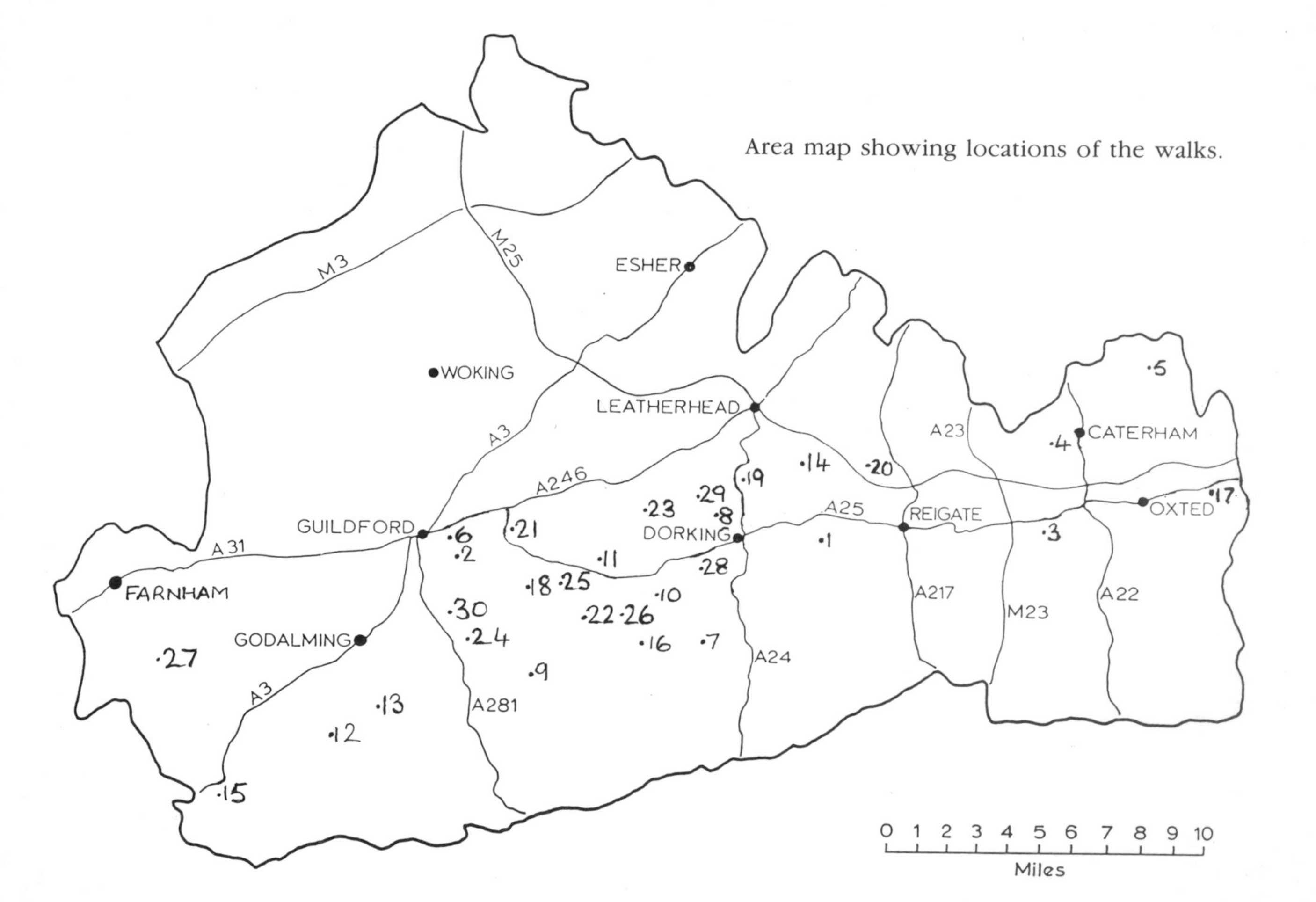

Area map showing locations of the walks.

Publisher's Note

We hope that you obtain considerable enjoyment from this book; great care has been taken in its preparation. However, changes of landlord and actual closures are sadly not uncommon. Likewise, although at the time of publication all routes followed public rights of way or well-established permitted paths, diversion orders can be made and permissions withdrawn.

We cannot accept responsibility for any inaccuracies, but we are anxious that all details covering both pubs and walks are kept up to date, and would therefore welcome information from readers which would be relevant to future editions.

Introduction

As someone who has been leading groups of walkers in the Surrey Hills and taking them into pubs in the area for the past ten years I had no difficulty in locating thirty that were suitable and devising interesting walking routes around them. The fact that I had previously visited all of the selected pubs, often quite a few times, in the past also helped to make my task more easy. Many of the paths used, but certainly not all, are ones with which I was already familiar. I hope that this knowledge of the countryside and the 'watering holes' dotted around it will be something you and your companions will be pleased to share with me.

In spite of its close proximity to the great metropolis of London, Surrey has some beautiful rural scenery and attractive villages where the march of time has not destroyed their tranquillity. Such is the vastness of the countryside, you may be surprised at the distance you will walk without seeing another soul unless, of course, they happen to be following the same walk as you!

Besides being blessed with more than 2,000 miles of rights of way, Surrey also has a few well-used long-distance paths running across it. These include the North Downs Way, now defined as a National Trail, which runs from close to the Hampshire border through Surrey and on to Dover. There is also the Greensand Way, running from near the border with West Sussex and across to Kent and beyond. A third path, the Pilgrims' Way, a route from Winchester to Canterbury, also runs west-east across the county. This is not an official long-distance path but is a historic route and frequently follows the North Downs Way. We use considerable stretches of these three routes, particularly the North Downs Way, since our aim was to keep close to the hills.

To complement the book the purchase of the two Ordnance Survey maps which cover most of the county, and certainly all of the areas used in this book, would be a worthwhile investment. They are the Landrangers 186 (Aldershot and Guildford) and 187 (Dorking and Reigate). They will greatly assist you in finding the pubs and the starting points of the walks, for which a map reference is given, and they will also enable you to follow the routes. If you enjoy map-reading and want to make your walk even more pleasurable as you go along, you may wish to invest in the requisite OS Pathfinder map(s), details of which are given for each walk. At double the scale of the Landranger, these maps show much more detail: for example, the side of the hedge on which the right of way exists and how the path winds its way through the farmyard. However, maps are not essential since the detailed instructions for each walk, coupled with the use of the sketch map, will ensure you have no difficulty in finding the way.

Contrary to a certain amount of myth, most pubs *do* welcome country walkers. Unfortunately, one or two bad apples spoil our image when they walk across the pub's carpet in muddy boots, expect meals to be produced out of a hat and, worse still, blatantly eat their own food on the premises – and that includes the garden, too! Nowadays, most pubs would not survive as businesses on drink sales alone and rely on the purchase of food at, mostly, quite reasonable prices. If you prefer to carry your own meal, please eat it elsewhere, and then enjoy your drink without feeling any discomfort.

All of the selected pubs, of course, serve at least two real ales – and some many more. The final brewing process of a real ale actually takes place in the barrel after it has been delivered to the pub. A good publican will tend the brew with loving care to ensure it reaches your glass in its very best condition. If it tastes as you feel it should, compliment the landlord on his efforts. In the unlikely event of it not being up to standard let him know as he will surely want to investigate any problem.

I experienced a considerable amount of pleasure in planning and checking the routes, many in the company of my wife, Brenda, to whom I am indebted for drawing the maps and checking the text. The amount of time devoted to discussing the pub – its history, its menu and other facilities – with the landlord or landlady, and sometimes other staff, too, was also a source of great interest and satisfaction. I hope that you, similarly, will enjoy good food, good ale, good surroundings and some great days out with the aid of this book.

Derek Palmer
spring 1994

1 Betchworth
The Red Lion

The Red Lion (Friary Meux) dates back to the 17th century and was a coaching inn with its own brewhouse, parts of which can still be seen to this day. Time your visit to the appropriate season and you will be able to see a spectacular display of wistaria around most of the walls. Nearby there is an unusual barn, one of only two of its kind in Surrey.

Inside the pub a beamed ceiling covers the pleasing bar with its tables for eating and drinking. In winter two log fires add to the ambience and welcome those coming in from the cold. This is certainly a splendid pub for satisfying healthy appetites, so try to work up a good one by taking the walk first. If you are really smart, you will book your table, particularly for Friday and Saturday evenings and Sunday lunchtimes. Children are welcome but dogs are not allowed inside.

In addition to the regular menu there is a blackboard selection of eight home-cooked specials. Taken from a range of 80 dishes, including local game, this menu changes twice daily. A speciality of the house are the exotic fish dishes but you need to book these in advance. The main menu is not available on Sundays but the blackboard will contain many options to satisfy all tastes and pockets. Complement your meal with one of the fine wines available or the real ales (Broadwood, Benskins and Tetley). Stowford Press is pumped for those preferring draught cider. If you are still feeling energetic the pub has the unique facility of its own squash court.

The opening hours are Monday to Saturday 11 am–2.30 pm and 6 pm–11 pm, Sunday 12 noon–3 pm and 7 pm–10.30 pm. Food is served on Monday to Saturday 12 noon–2 pm and 7 pm–9.30 pm, and on Sunday 12 noon–2 pm only.

Telephone: 0737 843336.

How to get there: The pub is on the Old Reigate Road which runs parallel with and to the south of the A25 Reigate Road.

Parking: There is an adequate car park which you may use whilst taking the walk, providing you are using the pub before or after and that you obtain permission.

Length of the walk: 4½ miles. OS maps: Landranger 187 or Pathfinder 1207 and 1227 (GR 214504).

The North Downs form a backdrop to this level walk which is mainly on open farmland, although you pass through a small area of woodland, too. The meandering river Mole is often in view and crossed at two points. Besides walking through the attractive village of Betchworth, with its historic church and stately home, you visit the village green at Buckland set in charming surroundings.

The Walk

1 From the pub car park take a path along the left side of the cricket pitch until you come to a fork. Bear diagonally right across a large field and past a redundant stile. Continue on an enclosed path between houses and come out to a road. Turn left. You are advised to walk on the right at first and then cross to the left at a bend, eventually joining a pavement. You reach Buckland Stores and Post Office and the A25. Turn right for a few yards along the main road to visit the church, with its 14th century window, a fine example of medieval glass, then cross over to enjoy the picturesque village green and its pond, old school house and church-shaped tithe barn.

2 Retrace your steps to the post office and continue ahead to reach the entrance of Buckland Lodge where you fork left. Pass a pair of cottages on your right and shortly reach Dungate Farm.

3 Turn right through a gate and pass farm buildings on your left. Go over a stile and along the right-hand side of a field to cross another stile and head straight across another field. The next stile leads you

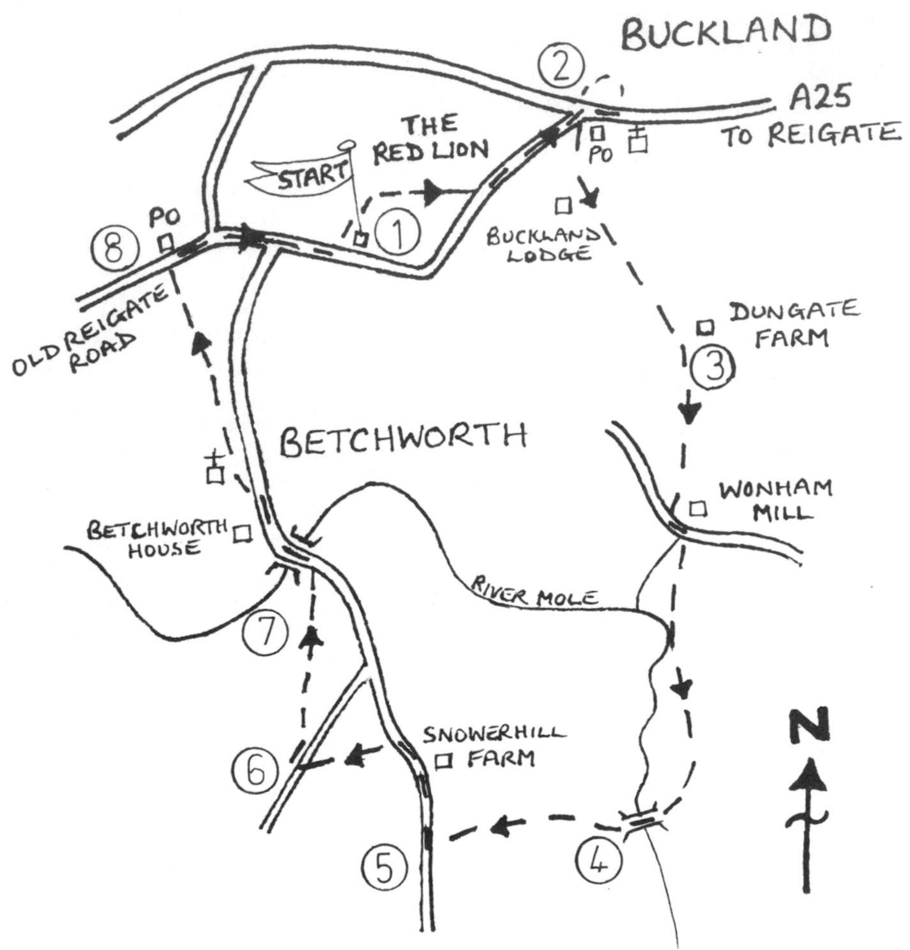

towards Wonham Mill with its pretty lake. As you reach the mill, bear right through a brambly area leading you to a gate and out to a road. Turn left for 50 yards or so and then turn right by a public footpath sign and cross over the river Mole. Shortly, go over a stile and into a field. Continue across the field, passing an old pillbox on your right. Pass the next pillbox on your left, with the river Mole still in view, then go through a farm gate. Continue ahead to pass a third pillbox and keep to the left side of a field. Pass a house, then a gate on your left and continue to the fourth pillbox. Is this where the invading enemy was expected to arrive? Locate and cross a stile, bear right and turn right, back over the river, then go through a fence and into a field.

4 Continue along the right-hand side of the field to its corner. From here turn right along the side of the next field, heading for a fingerpost. Turn left and continue along a track, passing the edge of a wood, then go through a gateway. In the next field bear slightly left, making for a stile by a gate, and come out to a road.
5 Turn right along the road for about ¼ mile and, shortly after passing Snowerhill Farm, turn left over a stile. Continue along the left side of a field, over a sleeper bridge and another stile, straight across a field, passing two oak trees on your left. Go over a stile and across a lane, then over another stile.
6 Turn right along the side of a field and shortly bear diagonally left across the field, making for a stile which leads you into woods. Go downhill to a ditch and a stile which you cross to come out into a field. Skirt the edge of the woods and then continue straight across the field, passing a solitary oak on your left, and cross a stile.
7 Turn left over a bridge, shortly passing Betchworth House on your left. Opposite the Dolphin turn left into the churchyard. Bear right, passing the church on your left, and go through the ornate lychgate. Continue on a lane past some attractive cottages and when this bends round to the road turn left through a barrier onto a footpath. Continue on the footpath leading to a school which you later pass on your right. Eventually you will reach a road with Betchworth Stores and Post Office opposite.
8 Turn right along the road and shortly pass a turning on the left, signposted to Betchworth station. Having passed a turning on the right, signposted to Leigh and Charlwood, bear round to the left and shortly you will reach the pub.

2 Blackheath
The Villagers

The Villagers (freehouse), just like the village in which it is situated, is of Victorian origin. Several years ago it was called The Volunteer and locals still remember the furore the change of name caused, some going as far as refusing to drink there. It is a pleasant house with attractive stonework and cosy corners in which to sit and relax.

Good, traditional food is the order of the day and the comprehensive menu includes familiar dishes plus two pancake choices, six different ploughman's, seven differently filled baked potatoes, soups and sandwiches. Special children's meals are also on offer. Besides the regular menu there are daily specials. If you are looking for a feast try the steak and kidney pie, or pudding, in Guinness. Various game dishes are available when in season. Almost all of the food is home prepared and cooked, as are about half of the desserts.

Regular real ales are Brakspear or the stronger Wadworth 6X and these are supplemented by at least two other guest beers. The draught cider is Strongbow and, in the summer, a barrel of Scrumpy is perched on the bar. Children, as long as they remain seated, can be in any part of the pub. Outside there is a large garden with woods beyond where children may play and where dogs are welcome. Bed and breakfast is available.

The opening hours are Monday to Saturday 11 am–3 pm and 6 pm–11 pm, Sunday 12 noon–3 pm and 7 pm–10.30 pm. Food is served on Monday to Saturday 12 noon–2.30 pm and 7 pm–9.30 pm (main meals only in the evenings) and on Sunday 12 noon–2.30 pm only.

Telephone: 0483 893152.

How to get there: Leave the A248 at Chilworth station, south-east of Guildford, and, in about ¾ mile, reach a crossroads where you turn left and in a few yards find the pub on your left.

Parking: The pub has an adequate car park but if this is full you can use the Blackheath Common car park which is only 100 yards or so further down the road.

Length of the walk: 5 miles. OS maps: Landranger 186 and 187 or Pathfinder 1226 (GR 034462).

Much of the walk is on the pleasant, mainly unspoilt heathland of Blackheath Common, a Site of Special Scientific Interest. Most of the paths are on sand and so there is none of the mud one usually associates with country paths after periods of heavy rain. You will have many fine views of the hills around without needing to climb them.

The Walk

1 From the pub turn right, back down the road, shortly going over a crossroads and into Blackheath village. You pass St Martin's church, reminiscent of a roadside church in Spain or Italy, on your left and, just before reaching the village sign, a strangely sited petrol pump. Just after the sign, turn left up a bridleway and, in just a few yards, turn right onto bridleway 307, eventually reaching a junction of paths.

2 Turn right, downhill, still on bridleway 307 and shortly reach a barn. Opposite the barn doors, turn left onto a narrow path (be prepared for nettles in summer). Later cross a low fence and pass some small oak trees. Go through a metal gate and over a stile, across a garden (the house is on your right), through a kissing-gate and then continue along a narrow path with a barbed-wire fence and a field on your right. You reach a pair of cottages and continue on a tarred driveway. St John's Seminary comes into view on the right and, as the driveway bears right, continue straight ahead through two metal posts and onto a narrow path (possibly overgrown in summer) which winds its way to a kissing-gate leading you out to a road.

3 With great care cross the road and turn left over a bridge. Re-cross the road and turn left onto a public footpath leading to Derryswood.

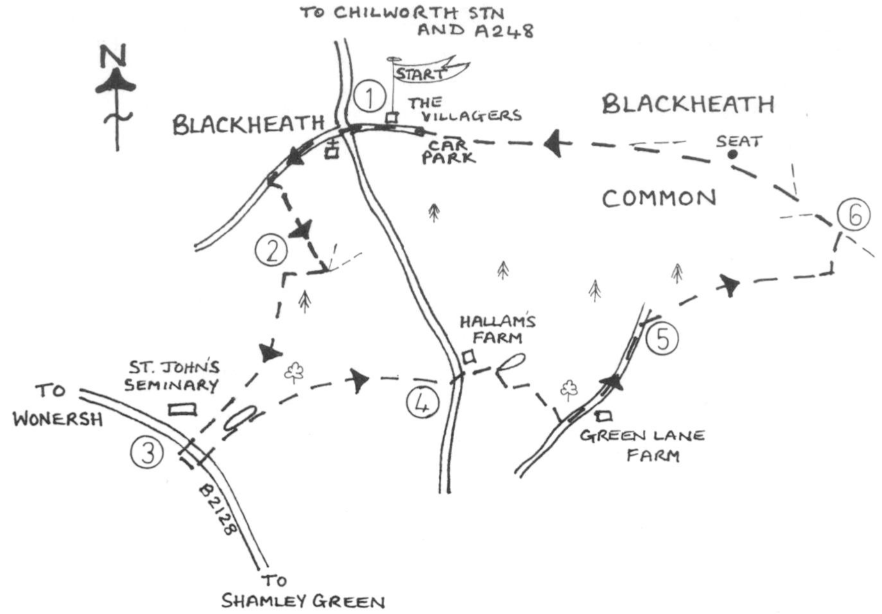

Pass a lake on your left and a large house with an ornate waterfall on your right. In another 100 yards or so go through a kissing-gate by a metal fingerpost. Bear slightly right across a field, passing two oak trees on your left. The path is not easily discernible here but you should head towards a stile to the right of a house. After crossing the stile, join a deeply cut path, later passing by some wooden gates. Continue on an enclosed path, passing a small lake with swans and rowing boats on your right, and later go over a stile. Once you are over the next stile, your path is no longer enclosed and eventually you come out to a road.

4 Bear left across the road and take the second turning on the right by Hallam's Farm. A metal fingerpost indicates a public footpath and this is also the driveway to Darbyn's Brook. The driveway curves right and left, passing an attractive lake with various wildfowl and a magnificent house beyond. After passing close to the house, the tar runs out and you bear right up a track, eventually reaching a lane. Turn left up the lane, shortly passing the stately Green Lane Farmhouse. The lane reaches a junction by a house and grassy knoll.

5 Turn right on a bridleway leading you onto Blackheath Common and in a few yards ignore a narrow turning on the right. Continue ahead, passing a mature conifer plantation over on your left. You shortly reach a junction of paths by a large oak tree. Continue straight ahead for a few yards and fork left. Later fork left again towards a house, then turn right on a small path running to the left of it, soon arriving at a T-junction.

6 Turn left on this wide track and, when you reach a fork by some wooden buildings, keep right on the bridleway. Ignore an immediate right turn to a footpath and keep left at a fork. The seat here is dedicated to Sir Geoffrey Hollis, the well-known Surrey author of several books and articles on country walking who died in 1980. Bear round to the left towards a junction of tracks in an open area. Take the middle of the three tracks, shortly passing a bridle waymark. At the immediate fork keep right, following the direction of bridleway 232. Go over a crossing track, no. 230, and then another. Shortly, join a wide track coming in from the right and follow this bridleway, no. 302, for another ½ mile to the public car park and the pub beyond.

3 Bletchingley
The Whyte Harte

The Whyte Harte (Ind Coope) is certainly the oldest inn featured in this book and probably one of the most ancient in the whole country, dating from 1388. It is, in fact, a hotel with no fewer than 12 en suite bedrooms, but has all the characteristics of a country tavern in the best English tradition. Obviously a building going back over 600 years has a chequered past which we do not have the space to cover here. On your visit request a complimentary copy of the building's well-documented history. The beamed ceilings cover several rooms which, in turn, have various nooks and crannies, so if the place seems to be full search around – you may be surprised where you will find somewhere to sit.

As you would expect from a hostelry of this kind the menu is comprehensive and at lunchtime you can have anything from a well-filled sandwich to a four-course blow-out. Besides the regular menu there are always four or five specials on the board. Most of the food is home-cooked and this includes the traditional puddings, too. There are always four real ales available, a regular twosome of Tetley and Burton with the others coming from a rotating list of ten. Copperhead is on offer for those who prefer their cider not to be dispensed from a bottle. Children may sit in the restaurant, which has a separate 'no smoking' room, and dogs on leads are allowed in the bar. There is a small garden where you can find shade from the sun on hot days.

The opening hours are Monday to Saturday 11 am–3 pm (coffee available from 10 am) and 5 pm–11 pm, Sunday 12 noon–3 pm and 7 pm–10.30 pm. Food is served on Monday to Saturday 12 noon–2 pm and 6.30 pm–9.30 pm, and on Sunday from 12 noon–2 pm and 7 pm–9 pm.

Telephone: 0883 743231.

How to get there: The pub is in the middle of Bletchingley High Street which forms part of the A25, east of Redhill. It can also be reached from junction 6 of the M25 via Godstone.

Parking: There is a small car park at the rear which you are welcome to use with permission, but you may also park off the road in front of the pub or anywhere along the cobbled forecourt of the neighbouring shops and offices.

Length of the walk: 5 miles. OS maps: Landranger 187 or Pathfinder 1207 and 1227 (GR 327507).

In an area dominated by the M25 and M23 motorways you will find some tranquil paths, mainly over open farmland but through shady woods, too. You descend from a lofty hill, the imposing site of a former castle, yet will be surprised to find you hardly notice the necessary ascent back to the start.

The Walk

1 From the pub cross Bletchingley High Street and go a few more steps towards the fine parish church, which is used regularly by the three denominations, Anglican, Catholic and Methodist. Turn left along the pavement which becomes raised above the street and in about 300 yards, opposite Castle Antiques, re-cross the main road to turn left down Castle Square. You reach a junction and continue ahead on a raised public footpath forming part of the Greensand Way, also signposted to Nutfield. Immediately you will encounter fine open views towards the busy M23 and beyond. To your right, although not in view, are the former ramparts of Bletchingley Castle, which was first recorded in 1160. Partway along this path you should discover a seat impressively carved from a tree which was, judging by the scorch marks, felled by lightning. Later, your path curves left downhill to a stile which you cross. Continue along the enclosed path which shortly goes into a tree-covered gully and then between fields. Ignore stiles to your right and left just before you reach some barns.

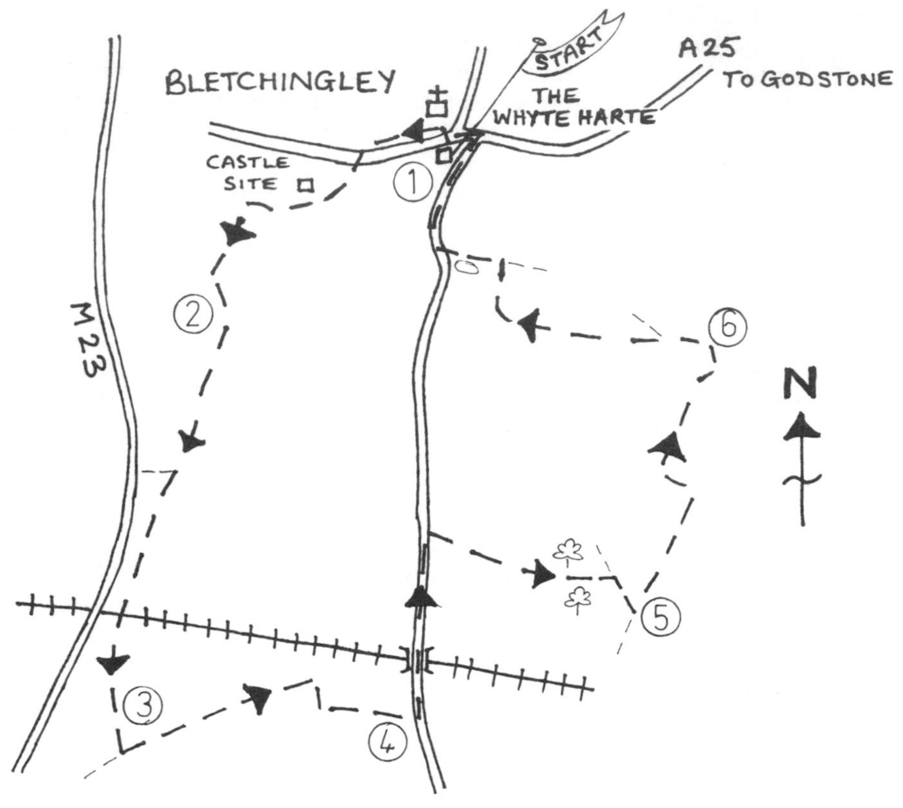

2 Bear right and cross a stile by a gate to continue on the track running around the perimeter of a field, still on the Greensand Way. The next stile takes you into a large field and you continue ahead on the tarred track. Later the Way turns to the right and under the motorway but you keep ahead, cross over a stile and continue along the right-hand perimeter of a field. Pass into another field as you get even closer to the motorway embankment and go over another stile. Maintain direction along the next field to a further stile leading you up some steps and, after stopping, looking and listening, cross a railway line. Once over the next stile continue along the edge of a field. Mercifully, the motorway bears away to the right. As the noise diminishes the tranquillity of the countryside may be interrupted by the drone of small aircraft coming out of nearby Redhill Airfield or by jets gaining height as they wing their way out of Gatwick Airport. Go straight over a field, heading for a gap between the farm buildings ahead, and arrive at a T-junction in front of Henshaw Farmhouse.

3 Turn left on a concreted bridleway which later becomes gravelled and passes a large concrete silage pit. Later still your track turns right and then left. As it curves right again by a house, cross a small stile and come out to a road.

4 Turn left along the road, shortly going over a new railway bridge. Continue along the road with care (the left-hand verge is wider but you may prefer to face the oncoming traffic on the right). Pass the entrance to Cuckseys Farm and continue up a slope. Immediately after passing the pair of red brick Parkgate Cottages, built in 1903, turn right on a signposted public bridleway, continuing by walking between fields. Later you enter woodland and, at the end of this, ignore a footpath turning off to the left. Bear right, remaining on the bridleway until it takes a sharp right turn.

5 Turn left over a stile with a yellow footpath waymark and continue up the left side of a field. Go over a concrete 'plank', then over a stile into the next field. There is a very round, very green hill over on your right and you reach a galvanised metal water trough. Turn left over a stile and go along the side of a field with a hedge on your right. You reach a metal gate which you will probably need to climb and then turn right, still with a hedge on your right. Pass into the next field and aim for the houses ahead. When you reach the houses, bear right, then left up a tarred driveway to reach a three-way fingerpost.

6 Turn left on the public bridleway and, when you reach a fork, keep left on the lower path. Ignore a right turn leading up to a transmitter mast and shortly bear round to the right. Cross a concrete roadway and keep straight ahead across a field. You reach a T-junction, where a small unofficial path ahead leads into a recreation ground, and turn left. After passing a large pond, which overflows onto the path after heavy rain, you come out to a road. Turn right and in five minutes or so reach the High Street where you turn left, back to the pub.

4 Caterham
The Harrow

The Harrow (Friary Meux) has young managers who bubble with enthusiasm over their first pub and exude the warm, genial personality associated with Merseysiders. Dating back to the 16th century, this attractive pub with its oak beams and flint walls is very much a meeting place for the local community but visitors, too, are made to feel most welcome, as are children and well-behaved dogs.

The comprehensive regular menu features unusual dishes, all home cooked and many a far cry from normal pub grub. If these are not enough, check the blackboard for the eight daily specials – four changing every day. There is also a separate dining area and, on warm days, the terrace is useful for those preferring to be outside. Real ale aficionados will not go wanting. Tetley, Burton and Friary as well as a guest beer are always available. If draught cider is your tipple, Olde English is on pump, too.

The opening hours are Monday to Saturday 11 am–3 pm and 6 pm–11 pm, Sunday 12 noon–3 pm and 7 pm–10.30 pm. Food is served on Monday to Saturday 12 noon–2.30 pm and 6.30 pm–9 pm, and on Sunday from 12 noon–2.30 pm and 7 pm–9 pm.

Telephone: 0883 343660.

How to get there: From the A22 bypass take either the B2030 or the B2208, which lead into Caterham. The pub is about a mile along Stanstead Road which runs south-westwards from the town centre.

Parking: There is a decent-sized car park which you are welcome to use whilst on the walk, but seek permission first.

Length of the walk: 3 miles. OS maps: Landranger 187 or Pathfinder 1207 (GR 327538).

Although close to a busy town, in next to no time you are led across farmland and onto an attractive stretch of the Pilgrims' Way and North Downs Way where there are some excellent views. This walk is on mainly level ground, so if you want to work up a real appetite why not try it in both directions?

The Walk

1 From the pub cross the road and turn left. In a few moments you should see Whitehill Tower through the trees on the left. (If you want to take a closer look at the tower, a late 18th century folly, also known as Arthur's Seat, turn left at the road junction for a few yards.) At the road junction turn right into Willey Park Farm and continue along the tarred track, part of the North Downs Way, for about ⅓ mile. At the top of a slope, where the track bears left, turn right off the North

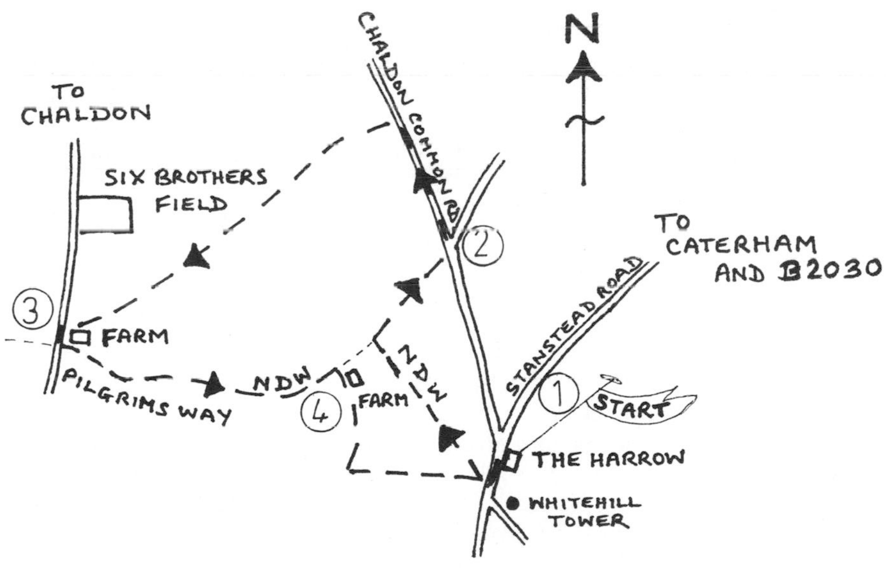

Downs Way and onto another tarred track which goes downhill for approximately ⅓ mile until reaching a road.

2 Turn left onto Chaldon Common Road and continue past an assortment of houses for yet another ⅓ mile until you find Birchwood Lane on your left. Turn left on this attractive lane, passing more houses and, later, stables. In about ½ mile you will reach a five-way fingerpost. Go straight ahead, in the direction of Hilltop Farm, on a brambly path for a few yards and cross a stile. Bear diagonally left across a rough field, heading in the direction of a short row of red brick houses. Cross a stile by a gate and maintain direction across the next field. The enclosed area over on the right is Six Brothers Field, managed by the National Trust. Go over another stile which is to the left of a pair of hawthorn trees. Maintain direction towards some old farm buildings and to another stile, which you cross, and then bear right through the farmyard, go over a stile, follow the path to the left of a conifer hedge and come out to a lane.

3 Turn left along the lane for just a few yards to reach a junction of tracks. Cross over the lane to enjoy the excellent view and then turn left at the entrance to Hilltop Farm and you are back on the North Downs Way. You will pass a sign indicating that you are also on the Pilgrims' Way. You reach an imposing house with a clock (Hilltop). Opposite the house there is an excellent viewpoint towards the M23 motorway with the South Downs on the horizon. Pass another North Downs Way acorn sign and, at a fork, keep right. Pass a bridleway turning to the right and, shortly afterwards, a footpath turning on the left. Go through a gateway into Willey Park Farm and you may find some interesting animals here – perhaps a llama or a Vietnamese pot-bellied pig.

4 By a fingerpost, turn right off the North Downs Way, passing between two houses and some farm buildings. Go through a gate onto a track and then continue on an enclosed path with a field on your left. At the bottom of the field turn squarely left and still follow its perimeter. At the next field corner you reach a fingerpost indicating that you are back on the North Downs Way. Turn right and immediately left to retrace your steps back to the pub.

5 Chelsham
The Hare and Hounds

The Hare and Hounds (Bass Charrington) is where the district's huntin', shootin' and fishin' fraternity meet and walkers are most welcome, too. Originally a grocery store, it has been a pub since the early part of the century and the locals are determined that it will remain so.

The menu, although not vast, covers most people's requirements and, importantly for those on a budget, the prices are moderate. Very reasonably priced are favourites such as soups with rolls, sandwiches, jacket potatoes, ploughman's, plus puddings for those who have room. There are always two specials and two additional desserts on the board – all good home-cooked food. If you time your visit right on a Sunday lunchtime you could be in for an unusual treat, as all the goodies on the bar are free but, be warned, they go very quickly. The real ales are Highgate Mild, London Pride, Charrington IPA and Bass. Children are not normally allowed in the bar. On fine days there is a garden with swings and other play equipment for them to enjoy. Dogs are not allowed in the bar and, even outside, keep them on a lead as the busy road is close by.

The opening hours are Monday to Saturday 11 am – 11 pm, Sunday 12 noon – 3 pm and 7 pm – 10.30 pm. Food is served on Monday to Saturday 12 noon – 2 pm only.

Telephone: 0883 623952.

How to get there: Leave Warlingham town centre on the B269 Limpsfield Road and you will find the pub on the left immediately next to the Sainsbury Superstore.

Parking: The pub has fairly limited parking which you are welcome to use whilst on the walk, but please ask first. Additional parking may be found outside the church behind the pub (not, of course, during services).

Length of the walk: 4½ miles. OS maps: Landranger 187 or Pathfinder 1207 (GR 366583).

Although bordering on suburbia, the walk soon gets you out into hilly countryside. These hills are not for the faint-hearted. Their ascents will give you a good appetite to satisfy and a thirst for quenching once you get back to the pub.

The Walk

1 From the pub, which is right on the Warlingham-Chelsham border, turn left along the main road, shortly crossing over and turning right down High Lane. Soon turn right again, along Plantation Lane, continuing on the main track straight ahead, with the valley down on the left. After just over ½ mile, the track curves round to the left and starts to descend.

2 Take the first stile on the left, then go straight down the hillside and across a golf course in the valley. Climb up the other side and, keeping straight ahead, make for a stile to the right of trees. Cross a road to a stile opposite and go straight up the hill, through a strip of woods, over a stile and out to a small residential road in Woldingham Garden Village. Continue ahead and, where the road turns left, go straight on between beech and privet hedges. Cross another small road, continuing forward on an enclosed path, then down a stepped path to a crossing track on which you bear left. Continue along the side of a valley for about ½ mile, enjoying a well-made path offering good views and with woods and one or two seats on your left. The last part of the path is fenced and eventually comes out to a wider lane on which you turn left for a few yards.

3 Almost immediately turn left on a fenced path going up a slope. You reach a residential road and turn right for about 100 yards then turn left on a path running between houses. You reach another

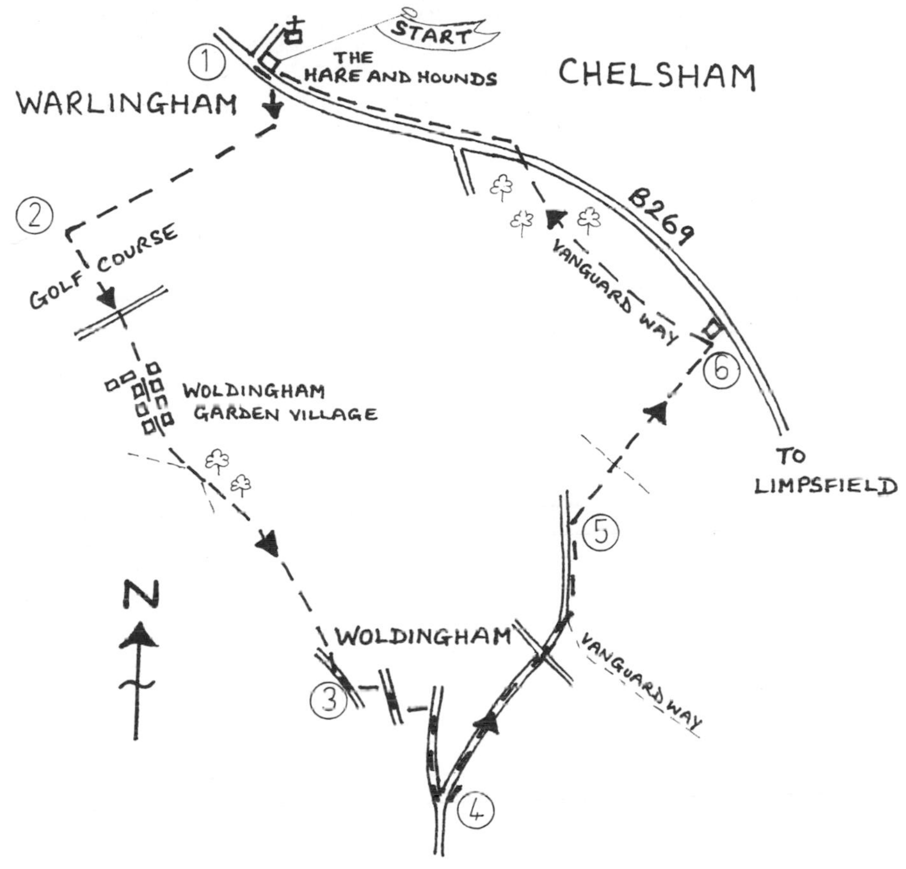

residential road and turn right, eventually coming out to a road junction.

4 Turn sharp left along Slines Oak Road. For safety, use the parallel road on the right at first and then take care as you continue downhill, over a minor crossroads, to where the road curves left. Ignore a right-turning bridleway but go over a stile and continue along the edge of a field, with the road on your left, for about 200 yards. This path forms part of the Vanguard Way – a long-distance footpath running from East Croydon to Seaford Head.

5 There is a stile on your left but you bear right, up a field, following a hedge and trees on your right. Your path goes down to a stile which you cross and then go over a wide crossing track and another stile. Continue with a fence on your right, go over the next stile and steeply up the side of the next field. Recover your breath as you go over yet another stile and continue ahead to the summit of the hill.

6 Just before you reach a house with a road beyond, turn sharp left and go diagonally across the large field. The path is ill defined, but follow a north-westerly course and you will soon come close to a pond and a disused pit which you should pass on your left. Also pass some horse jumps on your left and head for a stile leading into woods. Once over the stile, continue under trees, keeping right at a fork and passing a house with a flint wall on your left. You eventually come out to a road which you cross and then turn left. Keep to the footpath which, in about ½ mile, after passing a road turning and a pond on your left, will take you back to the pub.

6 Chilworth
The Percy Arms

The Percy Arms (Greene King) is a large, bright house with an attractive bar area and several interesting rooms. Parts of the building are 18th century and it has certainly been a pub for all of this one. Earlier this century it took on a macabre role when it was used as a mortuary for the bodies of men killed by explosions at the nearby gunpowder mills. Many old buildings claim to have a ghost and this one is said to be haunted by one of the unfortunate mill workers. A poltergeist is at large here and 'things that go bump in the night' have been experienced by staff and customers alike. No bed and breakfast here!

Important to anyone needing fortifying before or after their walk is the knowledge that they will be well served by an extensive range of good pub grub. The menu is comprehensive and on the blackboard you will always find three or four wholesome 'specials'. Real ales on offer are Greene King IPA, Rayments Special Bitter and Abbot Ale. If draught cider is your preference, ask for Dry Blackthorn. Dogs are permitted, as long as they are on leads. Well-behaved children are permitted without them. On fine days dogs, children and adults may enjoy using the large garden with its abundance of seating.

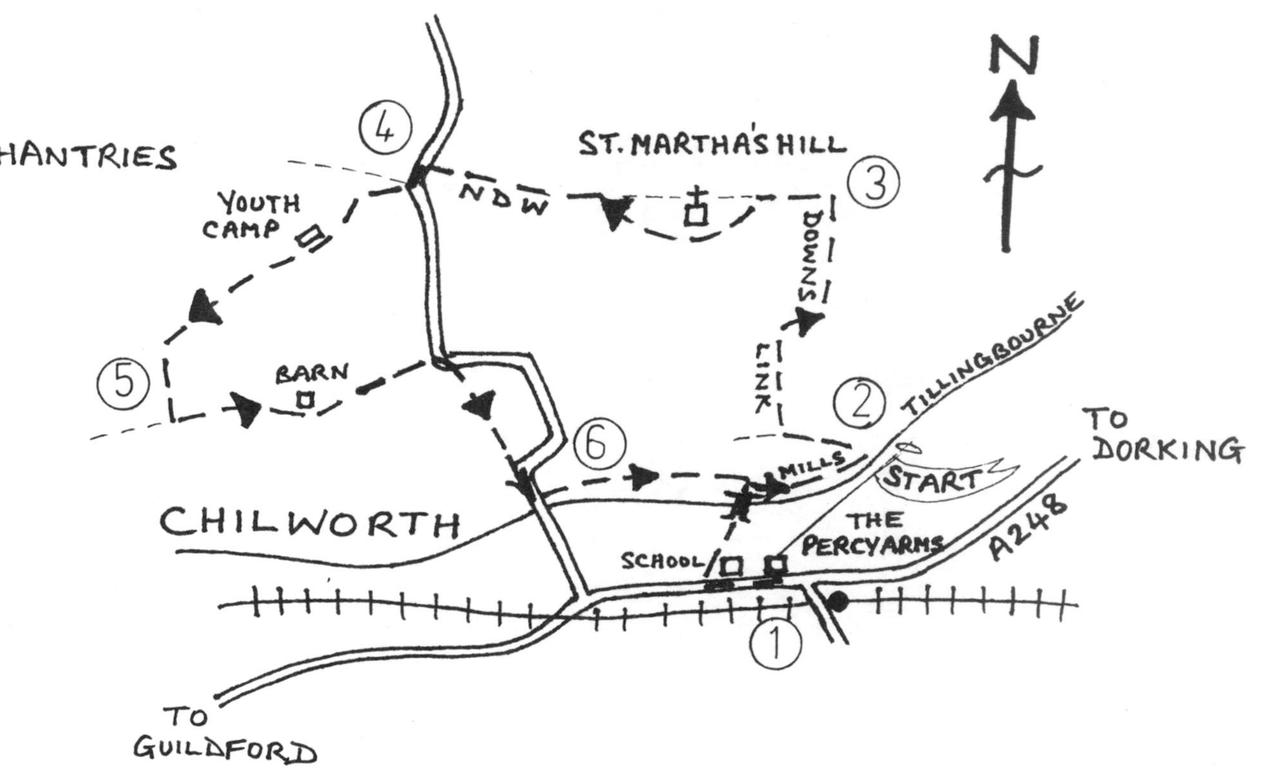
N
CHANTRIES
ST. MARTHA'S HILL
NDW
4
3
YOUTH CAMP
DOWNS LINK
5
BARN
2
TILLINGBOURNE
TO DORKING
6
MILLS
START
CHILWORTH
SCHOOL
THE PERCY ARMS
A248
1
TO GUILDFORD

The opening hours are Monday to Saturday 11 am–3 pm and 6 pm–11 pm, Sunday 12 noon–3 pm and 7 pm–10.30 pm. Food is served on Monday to Saturday 12 noon–2 pm and 6 pm–9.30 pm, and on Sunday 12 noon–2 pm and 7 pm–9 pm.

Telephone: 0483 61765.

How to get there: The pub is directly opposite Chilworth railway station on Dorking Road, which is part of the A248, south-east of Guildford.

Parking: The pub has a large car park and this is divided into two parts. Park in the farther section and let the landlord know that you are leaving your car there whilst on the walk.

Length of the walk: 4 miles. OS maps: Landranger 186 or Pathfinder 1226 (GR 131473).

Very early on in the walk you will be passing a slice of industrial history in the form of the Chilworth Gunpowder Mills. Guildford Borough Council has taken a keen interest in the preservation of this area and also the woodland of the Chantries, passed later in the walk. Most walkers following this attractive route will probably consider its highlight to be St Martha's Hill with its charming church and splendid views. It has always been a popular spot for locals and visitors alike.

The Walk

1 From the pub turn right along the road for a few yards and, immediately after passing a school, turn sharp right on an enclosed path. You cross the Tillingbourne via a bridge and fork right to a T-junction where you bear right. Pass a turning on your left and enormous, exposed tree roots and soon you come to the former Chilworth Gunpowder Mills. A little further on, stop to read the board giving detailed and interesting information about the area. You will now have reached a T-junction by a bridge.

2 Turn left along a track, continuing straight ahead past a right fork to a house. You reach a fingerpost and turn right onto a path which is shown as part of the Downs Link. The path curves round to the right and enters a gully, later bearing to the left. Your path slopes gently but the ascent becomes more steep as you start to go up St Martha's Hill. At the top you reach a fingerpost by a junction of paths and a pillbox ahead.

3 Turn left, leaving the Downs Link and joining the North Downs Way, with its acorn logo on a post where there is also a blue bridleway arrow and a sign for the church ahead. Where you reach a fork keep right, still on the North Downs Way. Your steady climb on the soft sand is shortly rewarded with fine views as you reach St Martha's church and its welcome scattering of seats. Having enjoyed the views, continue through the churchyard and maintain direction on a wide track, commencing your descent through pine trees. Continue downhill with a wooden fence on your left, passing an open area and a car park on your right, then go over a crossing track and come out to a lane.

4 Turn left down the lane for a few yards and then go right, through a barrier. Soon leave the North Downs Way by forking left, going past a sign saying 'No Horses No Bicycles'. At a fork keep right, along the main track. Ignore other turnings to the left and right until you reach a Surrey County Council youth camp where you may wish to use their 'facilities'. Now fork left, leaving the main track, and maintain direction along the more open, grassy hillside. You go through a gap in a fence and then bear left along the ridge of the hill. Go through an opening in the trees and bear left, still on the hillside, until you reach a grassy, steep slope ahead. Bear left down the slope, looking ahead for a narrow path which takes you through trees. You are led down to a stile which you cross, then turn left to continue between fields on a permissive path. Cross the stile ahead.

5 Turn left along a farm track which shortly rises and goes under a few trees. The track then descends and you pass some old barns on your left. Eventually you reach a farm gate and find yourself back in the lane that you walked along very briefly earlier. Turn right but only for a few yards for, after passing the driveway to Longmead, you immediately turn right onto an enclosed, public footpath. Go down a slope and back out to the lane. Turn right onto Blacksmith Lane and go over a bridge soon to find West Lodge on your left.

6 Turn left through a gate and continue on a woodland path, shortly passing a gurgling water outlet. Note some very large millstones on your left. In another ¼ mile or so bear right at a fork to the footbridge you crossed at the beginning of the walk. Retrace your steps along the enclosed path back to the road and the pub.

7 Coldharbour
The Plough Inn

The Plough Inn claims to be the highest pub in Surrey – and the highest freehouse in the south-east of England. This former coaching inn has traded as a purveyor of food and drink for more than 350 years. The tiny village is able to support a pub thanks to the vast number of people who drive through or walk in the area.

There is always plenty of good, traditional food listed on the blackboard, most of which is home prepared and that includes the puddings. Sandwiches are not on offer, but you can always have a roll with a bowl of sustaining, thick soup and the ploughman's lunches are substantial. The range of real ales is most impressive and the largest I have ever encountered. Members of CAMRA come from far and wide to tickle their palates with one or more of the ten ales which have travelled from various points of the compass, too. Be warned though – keep well away from the Bishop's Tipple and Old Thumper until after your walk. Something you hardly ever find in pubs in the South of England – mild ale – is also available, as is a 'winter warmer' in the appropriate season. Children may sit in the restaurant area and dogs may sit in the bar but not, please, the other way round. Accommodation is available and this comes with the promise of a breakfast feast.

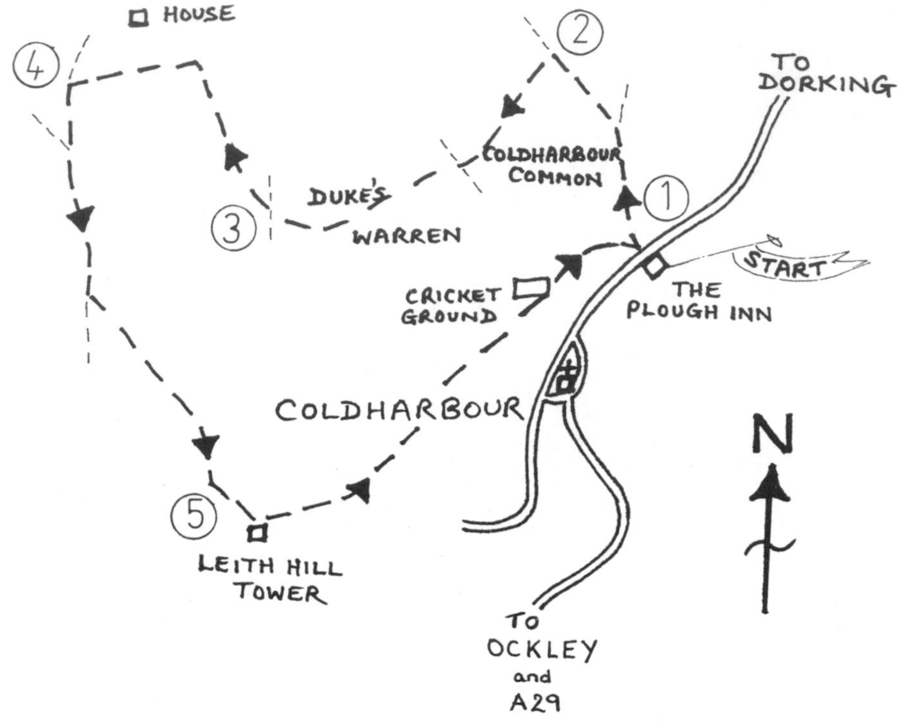

The opening hours are Monday to Saturday 11.30 am–3 pm and 6.30 pm–11 pm (summer) or 7 pm–11 pm (winter), Sunday 12 noon–3 pm and 7 pm–10.30 pm. Food is served on Monday to Saturday 12 noon–2.30 pm and 7.30 pm–9.30 pm, and on Sunday 12 noon–2.30 pm and 7.30 pm–9 pm.
Telephone: 0306 711793.

How to get there: Coldharbour is about 4 miles south-west of Dorking and is signposted from the town centre. It may also be approached from the A29, north of Ockley. Being well tucked away, it may only be reached on unclassified roads from either direction.

Parking: The pub has no parking of its own although there is a small parking area opposite. If you want to use the limited number of spaces you are advised to arrive out of pub hours, i.e. earlier in the morning or mid-afternoon, and visit the pub after your walk.

Length of the walk: 4 miles. OS maps: Landranger 187 or Pathfinder 1226 (GR 152441).

This is a wonderfully remote and fairly wild area which can only be discovered by those prepared to use their feet. Leith Hill, the highest point in the south-east of England, with its handsome tower, is a mecca for walkers, so do not expect to be alone when you are in close proximity.

The Walk

1 From the pub take the bridleway opposite and when you reach a fork by a barrier keep left. At the top of the slope you reach a metal water tank with two tracks forking left.

2 Take the first track on the left, waymarked as a public bridleway, and shortly pass a barrier and a National Trust sign indicating that you are entering Coldharbour Common. At the next fork keep right, following the bridle waymark. Later the path dips and you go between old boundary banks and over a crossing track. Keep ahead in a south-westerly direction and shortly go over another crossing track. Later your path starts a gradual descent in a north-westerly direction and, over to your left, you will have a fine view of Leith Hill tower which you visit later. Your track is joined by another coming in from the right and you continue on downhill.

3 At the bottom of the slope bear right over a sleeper bridge and in a few yards reach a plank seat. Bear left uphill, soon passing a 'footpath only – no horses' sign and going between wooden posts. Continue up the slope where damage caused by the hurricane of October 1987 is still evident. Later the track curves to the left and you have a view towards a large house on the other side of a field. Follow the barbed wire fence on your right until this turns right. Continue straight ahead here, passing through holly bushes. Go down and up a dip and, although the path may be obscured by fallen trees, if you press ahead you will eventually come to a T-junction.

4 Turn left on this rough, rubble-strewn track which shortly meets a smoother one coming in from the right. Continue ahead for about another ¼ mile, then fork left under stately larch trees. You ascend slightly and later go over a crossing track where your path becomes very sandy. You reach a junction of paths and continue straight ahead, later bearing left on the main track going uphill where you are aided by many exposed tree roots. Shortly another track comes in from the right and you still continue ahead towards Leith Hill tower. The top of the tower is over 1,000 ft above sea level and it is said that when the weather conditions are right, 13 counties may be seen from here. On a very clear day you may be able to glimpse the sea, some 30 miles away.

5 From the tower bear left and commence your descent. At the bottom of the slope you will see a deep gorge on your right, Cockshot Hollow, with a path running along it, and Duke's Warren in front of you. Take the second track to the right and shortly a right fork, following the red waymarks and 'Landslip Car Park' thumbpost. Your track forks towards a barrier and, after passing this, you turn left. You should be enjoying some good views over on your right with Broome Hall Lake below and the Weald stretching out beyond. Pass a turning on your left opposite a green-topped post, continue ahead and start descending once more. As you pass another green-topped post, your path starts to meander, and you will find more of these nature trail posts. Coldharbour cricket ground (the highest in Surrey) comes into view on your left. Shortly, join the wide track coming from the cricket ground and commence your final descent. It is worth stopping at the log seat commemorating the 1987 storm, where there is a fine view of the surrounding area. Very shortly you reach the bottom of the slope and come out to the road right opposite the pub.

8 Dorking
The Pilgrim

The Pilgrim (Ind Coope), a former coaching inn, takes its name from the nearby Pilgrims' Way. Although more of a town pub than a country inn, attracting local office workers during the week, it is conveniently situated close to an attractive area and sees many walkers on weekends.

Apart from the regular menu of familiar options there are also specials on the board which include more exotic fare such as Cajun chicken. Whatever you order, you should not need to wait too long as the kitchen is efficient and the service quick. Regular real ales are Burton and Tetley and there is always a guest ale. Also available on draught are Olde English cider and Guinness. Children and dogs are allowed in the pub and there is a beer garden with a play area.

The opening hours are Monday to Friday 11 am–2.30 pm and 6 pm–11 pm, Saturday 11 am–3 pm and 6 pm–11 pm, Sunday 12 noon–3 pm and 7 pm–10.30 pm. Food is served on Monday to Saturday 12 noon–2 pm and 7 pm–9 pm, and on Sunday 12 noon–2 pm only.

Telephone: 0306 889951.

How to get there: From West Street, which is part of the A25 through Dorking town centre, take Station Road, forking left towards Dorking West station. The pub is on the right just before the station.

Parking: The pub has a small car park which you are welcome to use whilst on the walk (please let the landlord know) and there is more parking available on the road or by the station.

Length of the walk: 3¾ miles. OS maps: Landranger 187 or Pathfinder 1226 (tiny part only) and 1206 (GR 161498).

You soon leave the bustle of Dorking as you head for Ranmore Common. A fine woodland path leads you down to the village of Westhumble and your return route takes you over Denbies Estate, the largest vineyard in the country.

The Walk

1 From the pub entrance turn immediately left and come out to a road where you turn left again. Go over the railway and pass St Martin's School, shortly forking left onto a public footpath which later runs along the side of a roadway. Ignore a left fork and continue to a road where you turn left. Follow the roadside path, which later becomes raised and in about ¼ mile, where you reach a gate on the left, cross the road to a public bridleway.

2 Bear right up the bridleway, soon ignoring a left fork, and continue to climb, with the vineyard down on your right. The track curves to the right and you go over a crossing track to join a part of the North Downs Way. If you look to your right you may see some fine stags in a field. You pass a white house on your left and reach a T-junction where you turn left. Ranmore's church of St Barnabus, designed by Sir George Gilbert Scott, is in view ahead as you soon reach a road where you turn right for about 200 yards and come to a crossing bridleway.

3 Turn right, ignoring an immediate right fork. Ignore all other turnings and, after about ½ mile, a track comes in from the right and you continue ahead. Shortly, you join a track coming from the right for a few yards before forking left onto a grassy bridleway. Later your path becomes stony and you start to descend. Go over a crossing track and continue with a field over on your left. Ignore a stile on your left as you go over another crossing path and reach a tarred track on which you turn left. Follow the track to the point where it starts to curve round to the left towards a ruined chapel.

4 Turn right through a gate onto an enclosed public footpath running between fields. Go through another gate and out onto a road at Westhumble. Shortly bear right onto Adlers Lane and later go over a residential road, soon reaching a crossing path.

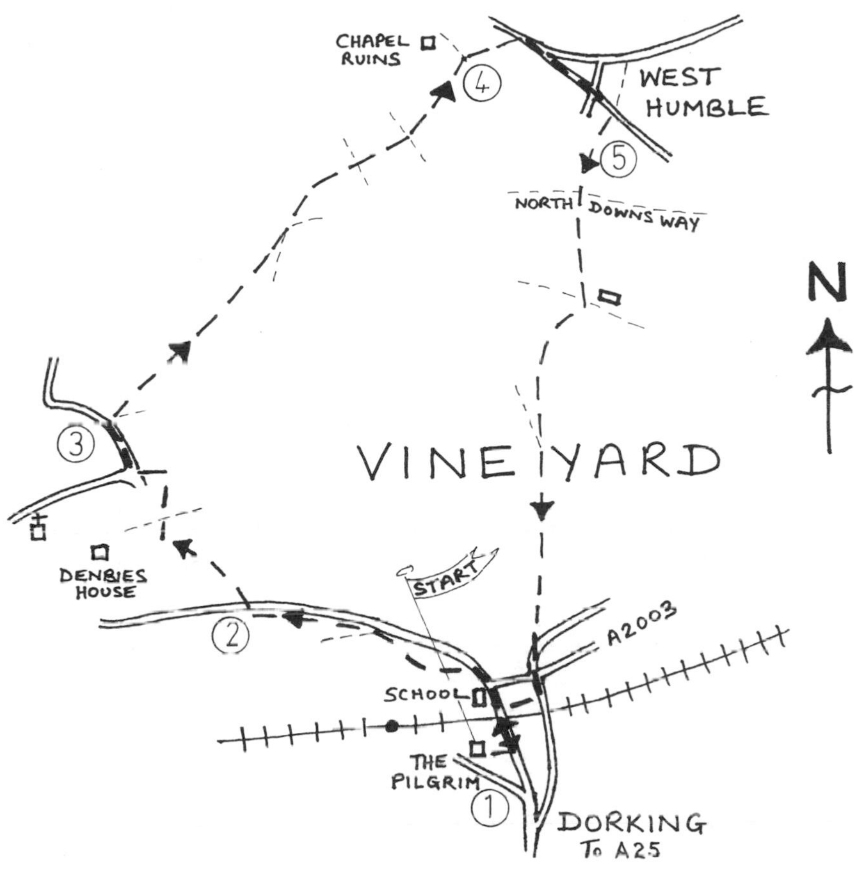

5 Turn right on the narrow, enclosed path running between houses and you are led to a barrier. Go across the narrow end of a field and cross a stile, almost immediately crossing the North Downs Way again. Go through a gate and continue on a wide track across Denbies Estate. Go over a crossing track. The vineyard buildings are on your left and there is a fine view of Box Hill, also on your left. A track comes in from the right and you continue over another crossing track. Eventually reach a gate and join an upward sloping track. You come to a grass triangle and bear right, down to a road. Continue ahead down Yew Tree Road to a roundabout. With care cross to the road ahead, signposted to Guildford. Immediately before a railway bridge turn right on an enclosed footpath and reach the road on which you commenced the walk. Turn left over the railway bridge and in a few more yards turn right, back to the pub.

9 Ewhurst
The Windmill Inn

The Windmill Inn (freehouse) must have the finest view a pub can offer in the whole south-east of England. Stare through the windows at wonderful, uninterrupted vistas, imagine you are in Scotland or Switzerland and then be pleased to realise you are still in Surrey. The pub does not have a great history, only going back a hundred years or so but, like so many in the area, was a haunt for smugglers. The false roof provided a useful means of concealing their contraband from the Excisemen of the last century. Quite a few management as well as structural changes have taken place over the past few years but the pub has settled down at last and is in capable hands.

The food here has always been a bit special. Whether you are sampling a bar snack, a bar meal or indulging yourself in the restaurant you should not be disappointed with your choice. Lovers of seafood should find something to their liking and vegetarians will be delighted to discover there is more than just bread and cheese. Well-kept Sussex Bitter, Young's Special and Courage Best come through the pumps. There is a lovely garden with plenty of space for children's play. Well-behaved dogs are welcome if kept on leads. Barbecues are held on summer weekends and you may also find a jazz band playing.

The opening hours are Monday to Saturday 11.30 am–3 pm and 5.30 pm–11 pm, Sunday 12 noon–3 pm and 7 pm–10.30 pm. Food is served on Monday to Saturday 12 noon–2.30 pm and 7 pm–10 pm, and on Sunday 12 noon–2.30 pm only.

Telephone: 0483 277566.

How to get there: Between Guildford and Dorking, leave the A25 for Shere and then take the road to Ewhurst. After about 3½ miles, you will find a car park on your left and, 200 yards beyond this, the pub is on the right. If you are coming from the south, leave Ewhurst village on Shere Road and find the pub a mile or so further on your left.

Parking: The pub has fairly limited parking which, with permission, you are welcome to use whilst on the walk. However, if there is no room you may like to use the Hurtwood Control car park just 200 yards away.

Length of the walk: 4½ miles. OS maps: Landranger 187 or Pathfinder 1226 (GR 080424).

This is a mainly woodland walk which takes advantage of the well-defined paths and tracks in the Hurtwood. It is quite hilly and provides a 'grand finale' with the fantastic view from the top of Pitch Hill.

The Walk

1 From the pub turn left, then immediately left again onto a public bridleway. If the weather is favourable you will now and then have spectacular views over to your left. In about ½ mile you will reach a road.

2 Turn left down the road for ¼ mile and then right, onto a public bridleway signposted to Winterfold Farm and other houses. Just before the entrance to the farm bear left, following the direction of the fingerpost. Bear right, passing the farm on your right, and come to a T-junction.

3 Turn right, soon ignoring a left fork, and continue on a track running between fences and going uphill through Jelleys Hollow. You reach an isolated house where you can take either the stony bridleway to the left or the smoother footpath to the right as both will take you up to a road. Cross the road and take the signposted public bridleway forming part of the Greensand Way. At a fork by a wooden post bear right, off the Greensand Way and onto a potentially muddy bridleway. You reach a crossing track, with horse-riding prevention barriers on each side, and continue on. In about 250 yards you will reach another crossing track by Wickets Well, one of several wells dotted about this

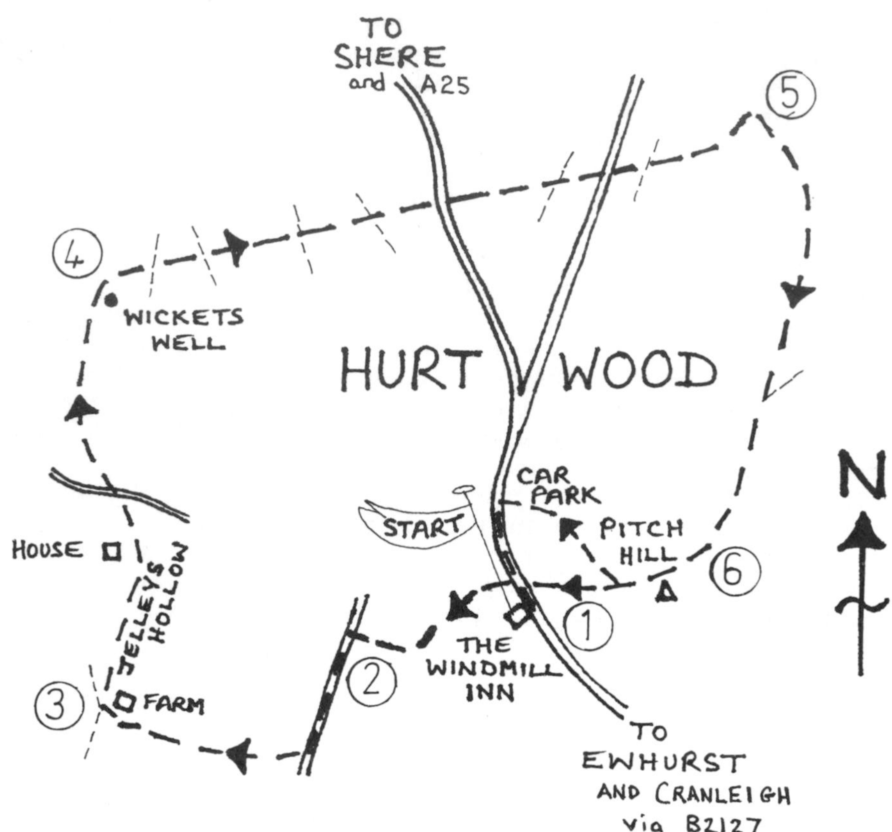

area and used, in the past, by tenants on the Bray estate.

4 Continue ahead through a barrier onto a public footpath which later bears right uphill and brings you onto a wide forestry road on which you keep forward. Go over a crossing track and at a fork keep left. Go down into and up from a dip. A wide track joins you from the right. You reach another junction of tracks and continue straight ahead on a narrow path. You are led through a barrier down to a wide track which you cross and then go steeply uphill on a narrow path. Go down to cross another wide track, through a barrier, up a slope and out to a road which you cross to the path opposite. In about 300 yards go over a crossing track and, about 200 yards beyond this, come out to another road which you also cross. Follow the direction of the public footpath fingerpost, continuing straight ahead and steeply downhill, aided by some steps. At the bottom of the slope reach a crossing track. Continue ahead on a narrow, rocky path which soon takes you over a sandy crossing track. Make your way uphill and at the top of the slope you reach a T-junction. Turn left and shortly reach a crossing track with an open area beyond.

5 Turn right onto a wide, sandy track which goes slightly uphill. Go over a crossing track into woodland, passing a Hurtwood Control notice on your left. The 4,000 acres of the Hurtwood are managed by the Hurtwood Control Committee with the aim of preserving the beauty of the area and the 'right of access by persons on foot for the purpose of quiet enjoyment'. Later go over another crossing track, later still pass a steep left turn and rejoin the Greensand Way. There is a metal seat on your left as you emerge on the summit of Pitch Hill, which, at 843 ft, is Surrey's fifth highest hill. Continue along the hillside, shortly passing a low wooden barrier on your left, and you come to one of the best viewpoints in the county.

6 Turn right towards a triangulation point, passing this on your left, then a Hurtwood Control sign on your right. In about 100 yards you reach a turning on the left. If you want the shortest route back to the pub turn left here but, be warned, this path is quite steep in parts. For a more gradual descent continue ahead, shortly passing a huge quarry over on your right. You come down to a car park and out to a road on which you turn left for about 200 yards back to the pub.

10 Friday Street
The Stephan Langton

The Stephan Langton (Bass Charrington) is named after the area's most famous son. He was instrumental in the drawing up of Magna Carta, being Archbishop of Canterbury at the time (AD 1215), and a copy of the document is displayed in the pub. Although it looks much older, the pub was built as recently as the 1930s on the site of another inn (see its photograph in the bar) which had stood here for centuries. It is cosy and comfortable with a welcome log fire in winter.

The dishes on the main, bar and special menus are all home cooked – and that includes the puddings, too. Being in the heart of the countryside, the pub offers locally produced game when in season. Real ales for you to try are Bass and London Pride and cider lovers will find Dry Blackthorn. Separate from the bar area is a room where children may sit with their parents. Dogs, as long as they are not too large or muddy, are also welcome. There is a small garden at the rear and plenty of tables and chairs in front of the pub.

The opening hours are Monday to Saturday 11 am – 2.30 pm and 6 pm – 11 pm (summer), 7 pm – 11 pm (winter), Sunday 12 noon – 3 pm and 7 pm–10.30 pm. Food is served on Monday to Saturday 12 noon–2.30 pm and 7 pm–10 pm, and on Sunday 12 noon–2.30 pm and 7 pm–9.30 pm.

Telephone: 0306 730775.

How to get there: Between Dorking and Guildford leave the A25 at Hollow Lane, just west of Wotton, and go south for 1½ miles, turning sharp left for Friday Street.

Parking: The pub has limited parking which you may use, with permission, whilst taking the walk. There is also a public car park which is on the right shortly before you reach the hamlet.

Length of the walk. 3½ miles. OS maps: Landranger 187 or Pathfinder 1226 (GR 128455).

This fairly easy walk, with just a few short climbs, from one of Surrey's most popular and serene backwaters, has lovely views from the earth bridge in the Tillingbourne valley. There are also wooded hills, plantations and farmland. Mud may be expected after rain, so go well shod.

The Walk

1 From the pub return down the road, passing Friday Street lake, one of Surrey's hammer ponds, and reach a T-junction where you turn right. Follow the road uphill and when it turns right continue straight ahead on the drive to Kempslade Farm. Just before reaching some white gates, turn left over a stile. Fork right, following the direction of a fingerpost, and continue on a path, with a wooded area on your left, until you reach a T-junction.

2 Turn right and continue along a path, with woods on your left and a field on your right. Cross stiles either side of a road and follow a wide path running between fences which later bears left, steeply downhill. At the bottom of the slope turn left over a stile and continue on a raised path which shortly takes you over the Tillingbourne and on to a stile which you cross. Turn left on a track and, in a 100 yards or so where the track turns left, turn right through a barrier on a path with a wire fence on the left. Go past the remains of a stile and bear right and then left across Wolvens Lane to a stile.

3 Cross the stile, head straight over a field then cross another stile, continuing fairly steeply downhill. Close to the bottom of the slope, go over a crossing track and down to a T-junction. Turn right, shortly going through a gate and onto a farm road. About 50 yards after passing the entrance to Logmore Green Farm, turn right onto a narrow, bracken-fringed path, pass a red house over on your left,

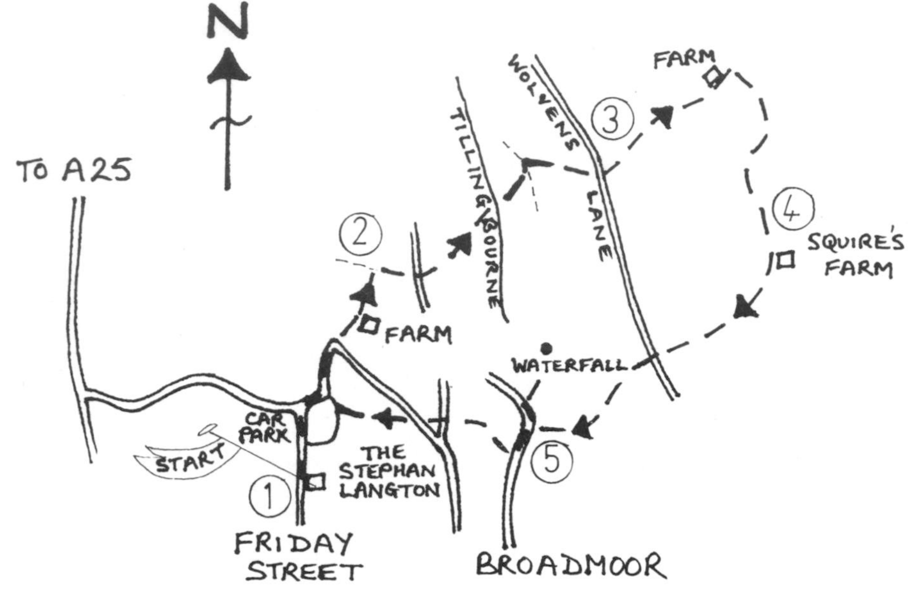

continue between fields, then beneath trees, and go through a metal gate. Bear left over a boggy area and continue along the side of a field towards a farmyard.

4 Go through the farm gate by a metal tank and continue straight ahead, passing Squire's Farmhouse on your left. You may find some guard dogs here but they should be enclosed behind the wire fence on your left. When the fence ends bear right on an upward-sloping path and, at a fork, bear right uphill. At the top of the slope you reach a junction of tracks and continue ahead over a wide, sandy forest road, climbing still but not for much longer. A wide track comes in from the right and you continue ahead, shortly passing a turning on the left. Cross another wide, sandy track (this is Wolvens Lane which you crossed earlier), shortly bearing left through wooden posts onto a nice, flat track. There are good views across to the North Downs on your right. Shortly a notice advises cyclists to dismount and you start to descend. Pass a house on your left and the entrance to another on your right. Go over a stream which feeds the Tillingbourne and shortly fork right. You reach a rough road on which you turn right and at the end of this come to a junction by some riding stables.

5 Here you may take a short and extremely worthwhile diversion to an attractive waterfall – about ¼ mile in total. To do this turn right and immediately bear right off the road onto a track and the waterfall is just ahead. Return to the stables.

Passing the stables on your right, take the road through the isolated hamlet of Broadmoor. Just before reaching a parish council notice board, fork right on a narrow uphill path and, after passing an electricity pole on your left, bear right, with the houses you passed earlier now down on your right. Shortly, you reach a fork where you go left, uphill. A wider track comes in from the right and you continue ahead. Following public footpath signs, cross a road and then shortly, another. Continue on the path opposite, running through Severells Copse, which will gradually take you downhill and past Friday Street lake. Turn left for the pub or go straight ahead to the public car park.

11 Gomshall
The Compasses

The Compasses (Gibbs Mew) was opened in 1820 as a beer shop, a forerunner of the 'bottle and jug' or off-licence of today. Drink was not consumed on the premises but people brought their jugs to be filled. The pub was extensively and tastefully refurbished in 1992.

There is an extensive and imaginative menu, with a children's section, plus four or five 'specials' every day. In winter months traditional food is served, particularly from the North-East whence the landlord hails. The restaurant has a no smoking area and children are permitted. The real ales come all the way from Salisbury. In ascending order of strength they are Wiltshire, Salisbury, Deacon and Bishop's Tipple. Draught cider (Strongbow) is also available. There is an attractive garden and to reach it you cross a bridge over the Tillingbourne. Barbecues are often held there in the summer. Dogs, under close control, are permitted in the garden and bar, but not in the restaurant.

The opening hours are Monday to Friday 11 am–3 pm and 5.30 pm–11 pm, Saturday 11 am–11 pm, Sunday 12 noon–3 pm and 7 pm–10.30 pm. Food is served on Monday to Friday 12 noon–2.30 pm and 6 pm–9.30 pm (bar), Tuesday to Friday 7 pm–9.30 pm (restaurant), Saturday 12 noon–2.30 pm and 6 pm–9.30 pm (sandwiches in-between), and on Sunday 12 noon–2.30 pm, with sandwiches only in the evening.

Telephone: 0483 202506.

How to get there: The pub is easy to find as it enjoys a prominent position in the middle of the village through which the A25 runs between Guildford and Dorking.

Parking: There is a small car park and you may also park along the road outside or, better still, at the nearby railway station.

Length of the walk: 4½ miles. OS maps: Landranger 187 or Pathfinder 1226 (GR 085479).

This fairly easy route includes a bit of a climb, with a more gentle descent, but these moderate exertions are made worthwhile by the splendid scenery. You start by climbing up to Hackhurst Downs, from where there are some of the finest views between Dorking and Guildford. You are taken over farmland, wooded and open hillsides and return to a delightful village, for which you should leave time to explore.

The Walk

1 From the pub turn left along the A25 and, immediately after passing a filling station, turn right onto a tarred driveway. At the top of the drive turn left to go through a wooden barrier and then maintain your original direction through trees, steeply uphill, until you reach a waymarked post.

2 Turn right to another waymarked post and then turn right again. Shortly reach a T-junction and turn right onto a bridleway, disregarding a backward-slanting, downhill path on the right. The track narrows and continues gently downhill, passing a grey house on the left. You come out on a small lane, signposted to Colekitchen Farm, on which you turn left. After passing the farm, continue uphill until reaching a junction of tracks at the top, known as Gravelhill Gate, where you may want to take advantage of a well-placed seat.

3 Turn right and follow a broad track, a section of the North Downs Way, for almost ½ mile. This is part of an ancient droveway, which was tarred during the Second World War for the Canadian troops stationed in the area. About halfway along there is a picnic seat and table at a pleasant viewpoint. When the track divides, bear right for a few yards and then turn right to pass through a wooden barrier onto Hackhurst Downs, still on the North Downs Way. Ignore a stile on your right and continue on, following the acorn signs. Disregard another stile on the right and shortly reach an open area with fine

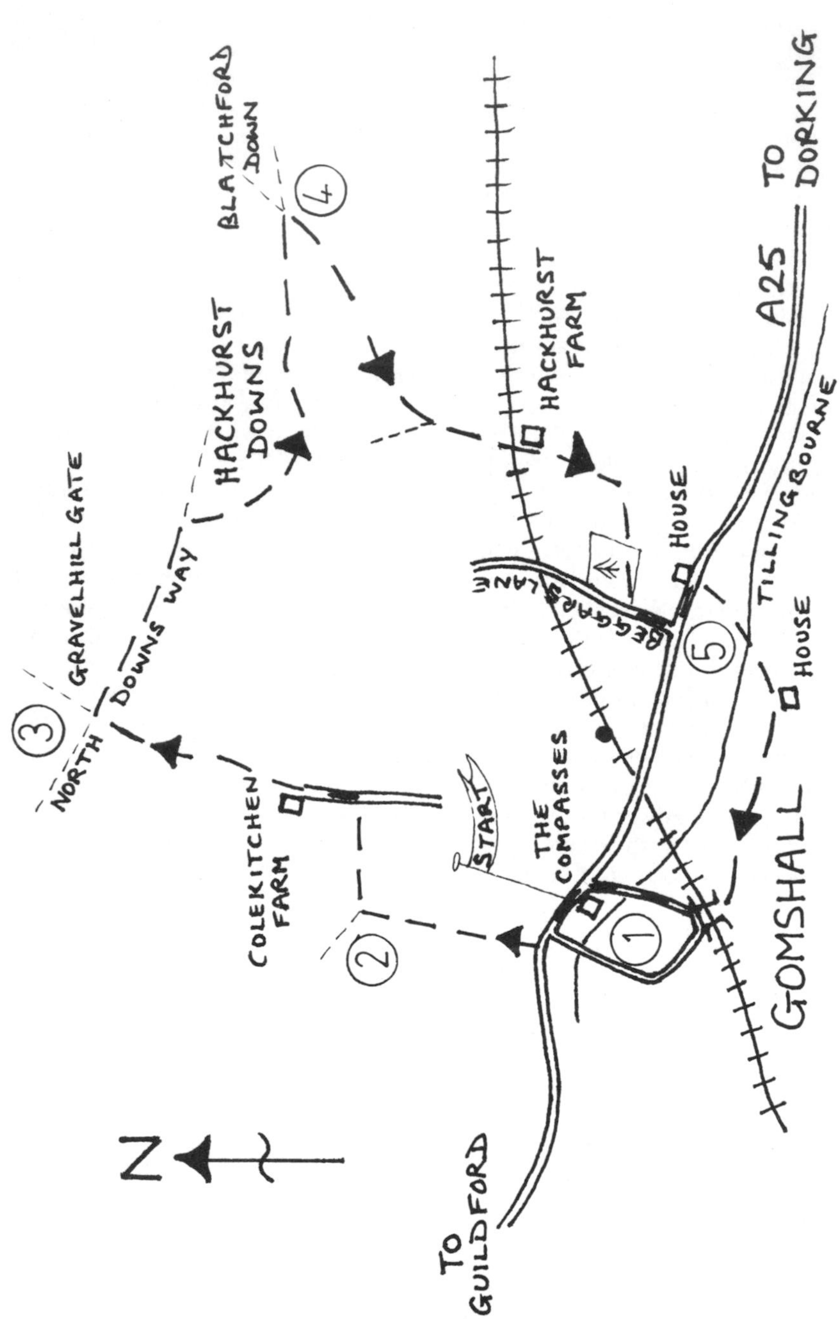
N
TO GUILDFORD
COLEKITCHEN FARM
2
NORTH
3
GRAVELHILL GATE
NORTH DOWNS WAY
HACKHURST DOWNS
BLATCHFORD DOWN
4
HACKHURST FARM
START
THE COMPASSES
1
BEGGARS LANE
HOUSE
5
HOUSE
TILLINGBOURNE
GOMSHALL
A25
TO DORKING

views over the valley below. Bear left onto a deeply rutted track and keep right at a fork. You pass a turning on the right and go through a kissing-gate leading you onto Blatchford Down, named in memory of Alan Blatchford, a keen walker and founder member of the Long Distance Walkers' Association, who died suddenly in 1980. You may find a herd of Soay sheep here. Grazing has been reintroduced into the area to help control the downland. Enjoy the excellent views over to your right and reach a stile which you cross.

4 Turn right and continue steeply downhill. At a junction of paths go straight ahead then, shortly, through a metal gate. Continue down to the railway line which you should cross with great care. Pass Hackhurst Farm and in about 150 yards reach a driveway on your right and go over a stile, following the direction of a metal fingerpost, along the left side of a field. Go over another stile and enter the National Trust's Piney Copse, continuing straight ahead. You reach a T-junction and turn left on an old road, named Beggars Lane, which leads you down to the main road opposite a vegetarian restaurant. Cross the road and turn left past a junk shop, continuing for 200 yards.

5 Opposite an attractive, walled Tudor house, turn right on a public bridleway. Pass some houses and go over the Tillingbourne. Just before the track rises, go half left, continuing on the bridleway slightly uphill, soon with a field over on your left. You pass Southbrooks Farmhouse and come out to a track where you bear rightwards. Just after passing a bungalow on the left, Twiga Lodge, the stony track bends to the right and you continue for a few more yards. Turn left through posts to take the enclosed and partly tarred path. Follow this path, which later runs alongside a farm driveway, out to a road. Turn right to pass under the railway arch back into Gomshall. Immediately beyond the arch, turn right and continue up the road, over a packhorse bridge and back to the A25. Turn left for the pub or right for the station.

12 Hambledon
The Merry Harriers

The Merry Harriers (freehouse) is a 400-year-old building which has been a licensed house from at least the beginning of this century – and it is a potty pub. To be more precise, hanging from the ceiling is one of the most comprehensive collections of chamber pots that you are likely to find anywhere. They have come from all over Surrey. If you are more interested in pop than pots look on the wall. A platinum disc for Status Quo and a gold one for Jethro Tull were donated by the stars when they lived locally and were regulars at the pub.

A mile away on the A283 the pub advertises itself as serving 'warm beer and lousy food'. In truth the food, whilst not claiming to be of gourmet standard, is hardly 'lousy'. It is good, honest pub grub (toasted sandwiches, baked potatoes, ploughman's, and so on) offered at very reasonable prices. The beer is not 'warm' either, but served at the temperature real ale buffs expect, Burton, Friary and Young's Special being the ones on offer. The ciders on tap are Olde English and Copperhead Dry. Children and dogs that keep a low profile are permitted and there is, in any case, a large garden with swings. Although there is no accommodation available, if you are travelling with a tent or caravan there is a convenient adjacent caravan site.

The opening hours are Monday to Saturday 11 am–3 pm and 6 pm–11 pm, Sunday 12 noon–3 pm and 7 pm–10.30 pm. Food is served every day 12 noon–2 pm and 6 pm–9 pm.

Telephone: 0428 682883.

How to get there: Leave the A283, south-west of Godalming, between Witley and Chiddingfold on the road signposted to Hambledon. The pub is about a mile further on. If you continue past the scattering of houses which form the village you will find helpful signs leading you through it to the pub at the far end on the left.

Parking: There is limited parking in front of the pub but plenty of space in its car park across the road. You are welcome to use the latter whilst on your walk, but please let someone know.

Length of the walk: 3 miles. OS maps: Landranger 186 or Pathfinder 1245 (GR 968391).

The route forms a neat rectangle on the map and covers a fair range of typical Surrey countryside. The climb to the top of Hydon's Ball is gradual and you are rewarded with the comfort of an impressively large stone seat and some pleasant views.

The Walk

1 From the pub turn left and immediately left again on a public bridleway. This track may be quite boggy after rain, so look for a bank on the left which will enable you to escape some of the mud for part of the way. After almost ½ mile the track bears left and you cross a sleeper bridge and reach a waymarked post.

2 Turn right on the public footpath and immediately go over another sleeper bridge. Soon you reach a junction of paths and continue ahead until you reach another waymarked post where you turn right. Shortly, go over a crossing track and reach another low post under power cables. Turn right and, in a few yards, go through a metal gate. Head straight across a field with Enton Hall over on your left. Immediately after passing a lake, fork right and continue along the side of the field. In the field corner go through a barrier and shortly pass a house on your left. Use a footbridge taking you over a stream and bear left on a pleasant path under trees. Later there is a deep valley down on your left and you are led out to a golf course. Turn left along the side of the fairway and, at the bottom of the slope, reach a crossing path.

3 Turn right and cross the fairway with care, shortly crossing another towards a large, wooden barn. Pass the barn on your left and

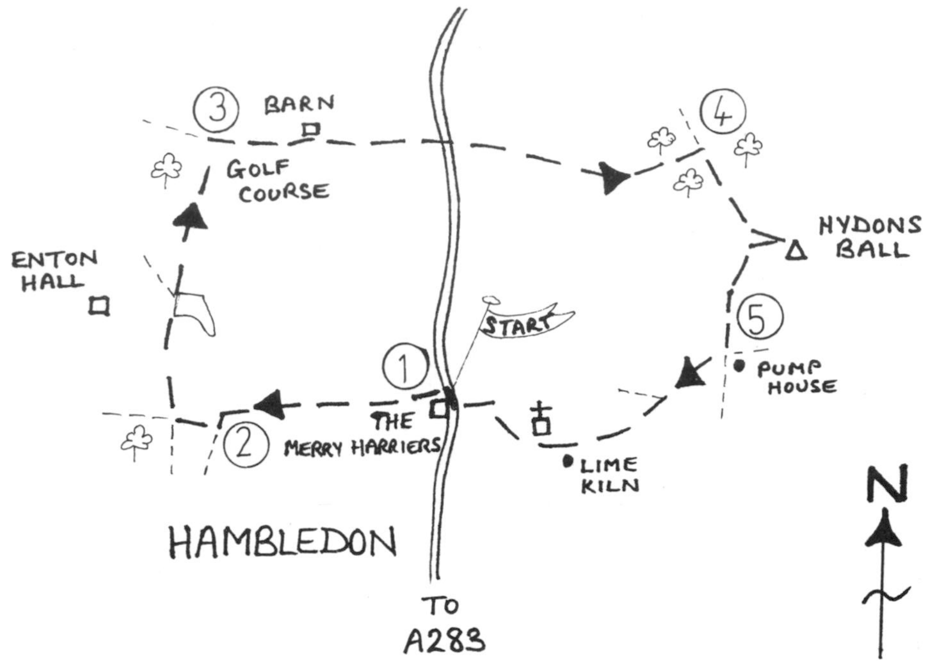

continue on the track ahead for almost another ½ mile where, after passing a small car park and then a house on your left, you will come out to a road. Cross the road and take the bridleway opposite which runs between fields. The track enters a plantation and starts to ascend. Later you will find a high deer fence on your right which ends at a crossing track.

4 Turn right, still with the fence on your right, and climb a little more steeply. You pass a green wooden gate, then another. Where the fence turns right for a short distance, turn sharp left by a gnarled oak tree and take a narrow path going through shrubs, which soon becomes wider. Pass some short concrete posts on your right and emerge onto the summit of Hydon's Ball, 593 ft above sea level, with its triangulation point and welcome seat. Facing away from the seat, and with the point over on your left, return to the path that brought you up to the summit but at the fork go left, fairly steeply downhill. Pass a couple of turnings on the left and, at the bottom of the hill, reach a wide crossing track.

5 Turn sharp right into another plantation, passing a brick pump house on your left. After about 200 yards, take a turning on the left which leads you down to a metal gate. Go through the gate and bear diagonally right across a field, heading for another gate by a solitary oak tree. After going through the gate, head straight across the next field in the direction of Hambledon church. Go through a gate and shortly look for an old limekiln, claimed to have been in use until the 10th century. You may like to visit St Peter's church and its churchyard and ancient yew trees. Continue down the road for a few yards. After passing Stable Cottage, bear right on a driveway and then continue on a downward sloping path. Pass some magnificent chestnut trees, turn left and shortly go through a kissing-gate and out to the road with the pub opposite.

13 Hascombe
The White Horse

The White Horse (Ind Coope) has always been a popular house with both locals and visitors. The building dates from the 16th century and was originally at the junction of two old roads, connecting Bramley to The Nore, which are now used as farm tracks and bridleways. The pub has a smart, new sign but, some time ago, displayed one painted by Gertrude Jekyll. She trained as an artist but is better known for the gardens she designed to complement Lutyens' houses.

Although busy at most times, the pub is well staffed so you should not have to wait long for your food and drink. There is a separate restaurant (more expensive) but the bar menu is large, with around twelve to fifteen dishes. Fresh fish, steakburgers and charcoal-grilled steaks are included in the home-made specialities, but ploughman's and sandwiches are always available, too. Real ales predominate and include Adnams Best, Friary Meux and Marston's Pedigree. The draught cider is Strongbow. Well-behaved children and dogs are welcome inside the pub and also in the garden.

The opening hours are Monday to Friday 11 am – 3 pm and 5.30 pm – 11 pm, Saturday 11 am – 3 pm and 6 pm – 11 pm and Sunday 12 noon – 3 pm and 7 pm – 10.30 pm. Food is served on Monday to

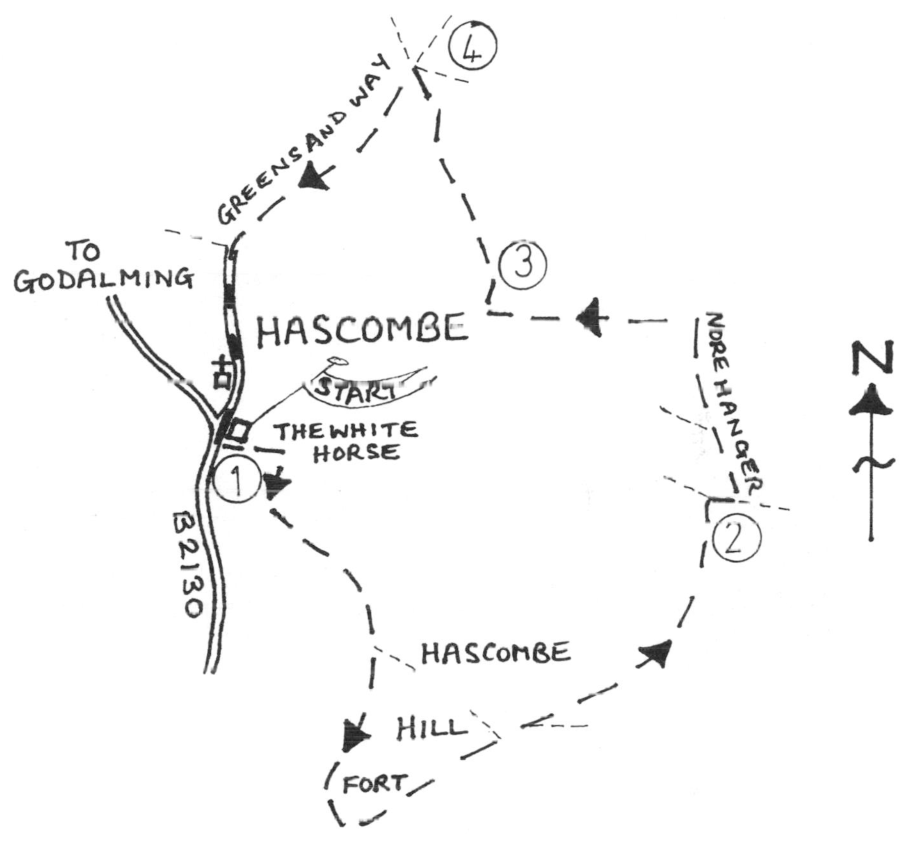

Saturday 12 noon–2.15 pm and 7 pm–10 pm, and on Sunday 12 noon–2.15 pm and 7 pm–9.30 pm.

Telephone: 048 632 258.

How to get there: The pub is just south of Hascombe, on the B2130, and about 3½ miles from Godalming.

Parking: There is a large car park which you may use, with permission, whilst on your walk. If this is full look for a space on the grassy verge across the road.

Length of the walk: 3 miles. OS maps: Landranger 186 or Pathfinder 1226 and 1246 (GR 002394).

You are soon on Hascombe Hill, with its encircling path giving you excellent views in several directions. The final few yards of the walk take you through part of the attractive village with its large pond and appealing houses.

The Walk

1 From the pub turn left and left again onto a bridleway going alongside it. In about 100 yards turn right, past a wooden garage marked Hascombe Place Farm. Go over a stile onto a track in a deep gully. You shortly reach a fork and keep left, commencing your ascent of Hascombe Hill. A track soon comes in from your right. Climb steadily to the next fork where you go right and your path becomes enclosed by rhododendron bushes. You meet a junction of paths by some mighty beech trees and bear right, continuing round the contour of the hill. The views start to open out, thanks mainly to the October 1987 hurricane when trees along the side of the path were blown down. As you continue to curve round the hill, the views become even more expansive as you look south across the Weald towards the South Downs on the horizon. At one point you may spot aircraft sitting by the runways of Dunsfold Airfield and above you on the left is the site of an Iron Age fort and the summit at 644 ft. As you wind round the hill in a north-easterly direction you pass a turning on the left and, a few yards beyond this, come to a well-defined fork where you keep left on the higher path. The hillside still runs steeply down on your right and later the path starts to descend as you pass the remains of a metal fence on your right. The dense woodland is mainly beech and chestnut. Eventually you pass a fence and field on your left and reach a T-junction by the remains of a barrier.

2 Turn right on a deep path for 50 yards or so where you turn left through a raised avenue of beeches. Nore Hanger is down on your right and on the skyline you have good views towards Holmbury, Pitch and Leith Hills. At a fork keep right and about 250 yards beyond this, at the next junction, turn left. Eventually this narrow path, with a steep wooded slope down on your right, meets a T-junction where you turn right on a wider path. In another 200 yards take a right turn and in a few yards more turn right again towards a broken stile, which you do not cross.

3 Fork left onto a narrow path with a wire fence on the right and brambles on the left. This path becomes wider as it winds its way under trees and, later, through a coppiced woodland. A track comes in from the right by a gate and you reach a more open area and a crossing track.

4 Turn left on this wide track which forms part of the Greensand Way and you will eventually reach a large wooden barn. A few yards beyond the barn, fork right, away from the main track, onto a signed bridleway. Your path starts to descend and becomes quite rough and stony in parts, although later you are aided by an occasional step. You reach some houses and a tarred driveway which leads down to a narrow road where you bear left. Continue along the road, with a stream down on your right, later bearing right to the pond in Hascombe, with its pleasant surrounding green and seats. Pass St Peter's church on your right and in a few more yards you will be back at the pub.

14 Headley
The Cock Inn

The Cock Inn (Friary Meux) looks like a nice new modern pub but part of it, the public bar (a rarity these days), was a bakehouse and dates from the 16th century. The saloon bar, complete with open fire in winter, is cosy and there is also a large dining area.

Most of the food is home cooked and the prices are reasonable. Fresh cod with home-made batter is a firm favourite amongst regulars but those requiring something lighter will find such things as jacket potatoes, filled rolls and soups. There is an extensive menu, plus specials which include a home-made vegetarian dish. Lunchtime on Sundays has specials only, including a roast, but there is no food in the evening. You will find Burton Ale, Friary Meux Bitter, Benskins Bitter and Tetley, plus Olde English cider. In addition there is a guest ale which changes every two weeks. Outside is a beer garden where dogs and children are permitted. Dogs are also allowed in the bar only, and children in the restaurant area.

The opening hours are Monday to Friday 11 am–2.30 pm and 6 pm–11 pm, Saturday 11 am–3 pm and 6 pm–11 pm, Sunday 12 noon–3 pm and 7 pm–10.30 pm. Food is served on Monday to Saturday 12 noon–2 pm and 6.30 pm–9.15 pm, and on Sunday 12 noon–2.15 pm only.

Telephone: 0372 377258.

How to get there: Headley is 2 miles east of the A24 at Leatherhead, via the B2033. At the T-junction in the village, turn left for ½ mile to the pub, which is on the right just before the church.

Parking: The pub has a large car park which you are welcome to use, with permission, whilst on the walk. It tends to be full at weekends but there is additional parking by the adjacent church. Alternatively, use the Headley Heath car park, free to National Trust members, which requires a right turn at the T-junction in Headley (and is passed on the walk).

Length of the walk: 4 miles. OS maps: Landranger 187 or Pathfinder 1206 and 1207 (GR 170517).

Headley Heath, with its profusion of heather, is a wonderfully hilly, open space with panoramic views. Always popular with ramblers, dog walkers and horse riders, it is a fine area to visit at any time of the year but in late summer the heather is at its best and in early autumn the trees burst into a symphony of colour.

The Walk

1 From the pub turn right towards the church. Go through the gate into the churchyard and at the church door turn right and then left to go through the combined lych and kissing gate. Turn right, going over a stile and a crossing bridleway. Go over another stile and across a field, then over two more stiles by The Old Rectory. Continue over the next field and stile and finally reach a metal three-way fingerpost.

2 Turn right over a stile and continue along an enclosed path with a pleasing view of the church over on your right. You come out onto a driveway and bear right to a T-junction where you turn left. Go through a wooden barrier to take the path running parallel with the road on your right. You reach a tarred driveway and turn right and then left, crossing the road onto a narrow path by an ivy-clad tree. In about 150 yards at a T-junction, turn left and shortly ignore a right turn. Walk along the edge of a car park and, immediately after passing it, turn left on a wide track for a few yards and then turn right onto a narrow one going under trees. You reach a junction of paths and there is a seat over on your left. Bear left for a few yards and then go right, onto the main bridleway. (There is another bridleway running parallel on your left.) Later go over a crossing track, passing a 'no horses' sign on your left. The track bears round to the right and you pass a pond on your right. Pass a National Trust Long Walk (NTLW) sign on your left and reach a crossing track.

3 Turn right in the direction of the NTLW arrow and, when you reach another junction of paths, bear left, still following the NTLW

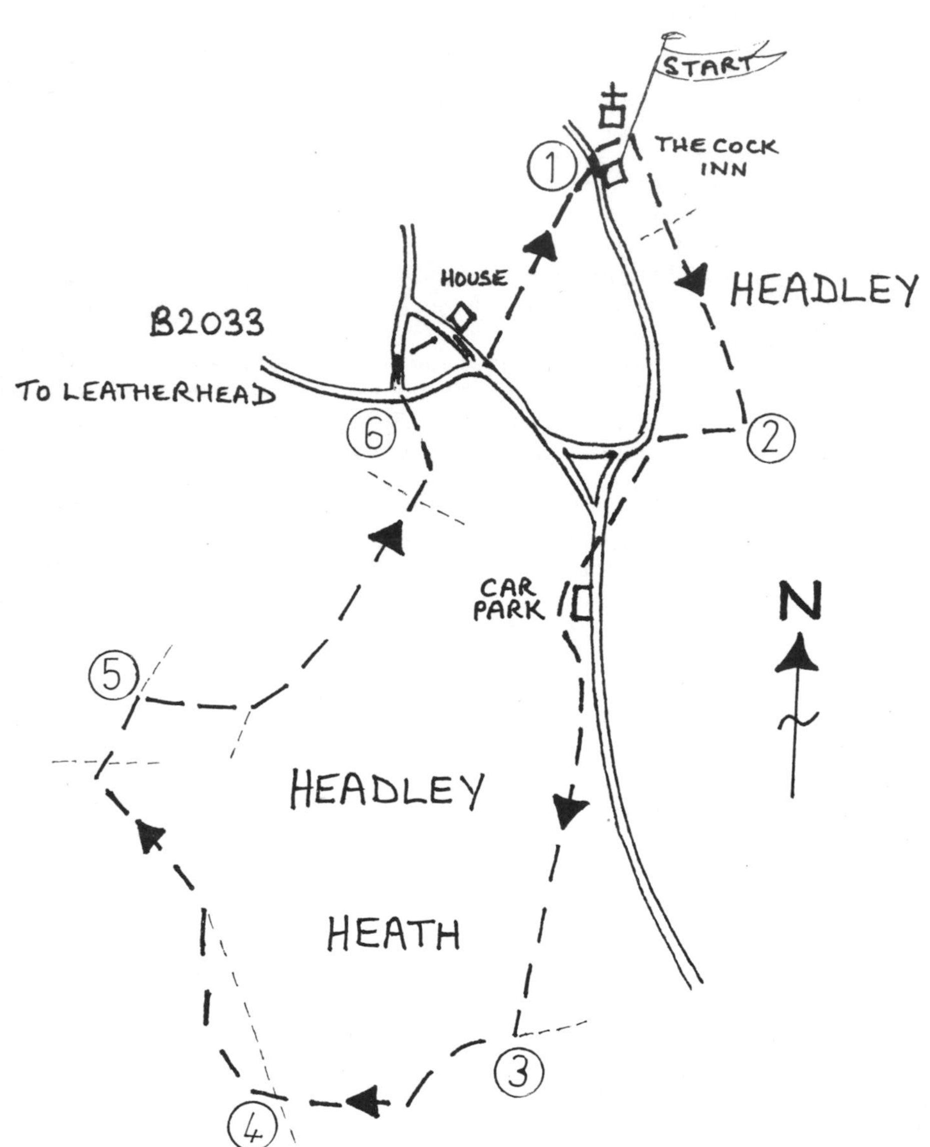
START
THE COCK INN
1
HOUSE
HEADLEY
B2033
TO LEATHERHEAD
6
2
CAR PARK
N
5
HEADLEY
HEATH
3
4

sign. The track curves down to the right and you then bear right, no longer following the NTLW arrows. Shortly reach a crossing track and turn left, passing a 'no horses' sign, and soon reach a junction of many paths.

4 Go straight ahead on a grassy path, which later bears round to the right. There is an open area on your right and later on one on your left. Eventually you reach a solitary oak tree by a seat with a dedication where another track comes in from the right. Continue straight ahead. There are spectacular views as you start to descend, passing more seats on your left. At the bottom of the slope you go through a metal barrier to a T-junction. Turn right for a few yards and then turn left back onto a NTLW trail and climb a long flight of steps. At the top you reach a welcome seat where you may wish to recover your breath and take in the views.

5 Turn right with the NTLW sign and proceed along the ridge path, later passing another NTLW sign. At the next NTLW sign, fork left to a crossing track where you turn left. Your gravelly path goes down and up a couple of times and takes you over some narrow crossing tracks. The gravel gives way to sand and you reach a junction where the main track goes round to the right, but you continue straight ahead passing a dip on your right. Pass a house and come out to a road.

6 Cross the road to the lane opposite (Tumber Street) and in about 100 yards, immediately you are over the top of a slope, turn right, into woods. At a fork keep right to reach a small parking area in front of a large white house. Turn right to the road and then immediately left on an enclosed footpath to the left of Ash House. Continue along the path between paddocks and shortly Headley church and the pub come into view.

15 Hindhead
The Devils Punchbowl Hotel

The Devils Punchbowl Hotel (freehouse) is, at 850 ft above sea level, the highest in south-east England. It is a smart, three-star hotel, with 40 en suite rooms, and its Russell's Bar is popular with hotel guests, village locals and passing ramblers. The original part of the building goes back to the late 1880s when Hindhead became a mecca for health-seeking Victorian society. Almost overlooking the famous Devil's Punch Bowl itself, the hotel sits in the centre of an outstanding area for good, healthy exercise.

Russell's Bar has a mouth-watering list of meals for the hungry walker, with prices that will not break the bank. The fare ranges from sandwiches, made from fresh, crusty bread, and ploughman's to salads and main meals. Vegetarians are well looked after, too, with three or four pleasing choices. There is an impressive line of pumps dispensing some of the South-East's finest beers, including Badger, Wadworth 6X, Tanglefoot and Courage Best. Or there is Dry Blackthorn cider for those who prefer it. Children are welcome but, with so many people eating here, dogs are best left in the car.

The opening hours are Monday to Saturday 11 am–3 pm and

5.30 pm – 11 pm, and Sunday 12 noon – 3 pm and 7 pm – 10.30 pm. Food is served every day 12 noon – 2.30 pm and 6.30 pm – 10 pm.
Telephone: 0428 606565.

How to get there: You cannot miss the hotel which, if you are travelling south, is on the left of the A3 London – Portsmouth road just as you enter Hindhead.

Parking: The hotel has a large car park which you are welcome to use whilst on the walk. If this is full there is an even larger National Trust car park on the other side of the road.

Length of the walk: 4 miles. OS maps: Landranger 186 or Pathfinder 1245 (GR 890356).

This is a very fine area for walking and one of the most beautiful owned by the National Trust. On clear days the views from Gibbett Hill are spectacular. Towards the end of this boot shaped route, you are taken to the famous Surrey beauty spot, the Devil's Punch Bowl.

The Walk

1 From the hotel turn right along the main road. Ignore a public footpath turning immediately right and continue a few yards, bearing right under a metal barrier and onto a wide track. Your path forms part of the Greensand Way and, ignoring all turnings, you remain on it for over ¼ mile where you will reach a fork by a seat. Bear left and soon join a track coming from the right. Shortly, you reach a junction of paths and maintain your north-easterly direction. Before reaching a car park ahead, take a left fork and reach another junction.

2 Turn left for a short diversion. In about 100 yards you will find the Sailor's Stone on your right, marking the spot where, in 1786, a lone sailor on his way to Portsmouth was murdered by three ruffians. The inscription on the stone warns you of the curse laid on anyone who tries to move it. Retrace your steps and go through the car park, continuing to the edge of Gibbet Hill with its seats, triangulation point and the granite cross which marks the site of the former gibbet. The hill, at 895 ft, is the second highest in Surrey (next to Leith Hill) and the third highest in south-east England, beaten by Blackdown in West Sussex. By the cross take a narrow path going right (Greensand Way) and then go through a wooden barrier. Turn left down to another track on which you bear right. You are now walking on the Old Portsmouth Road. Remain on this, ignoring a couple of left forks, and eventually come down to the A3 which you should cross with very great care.

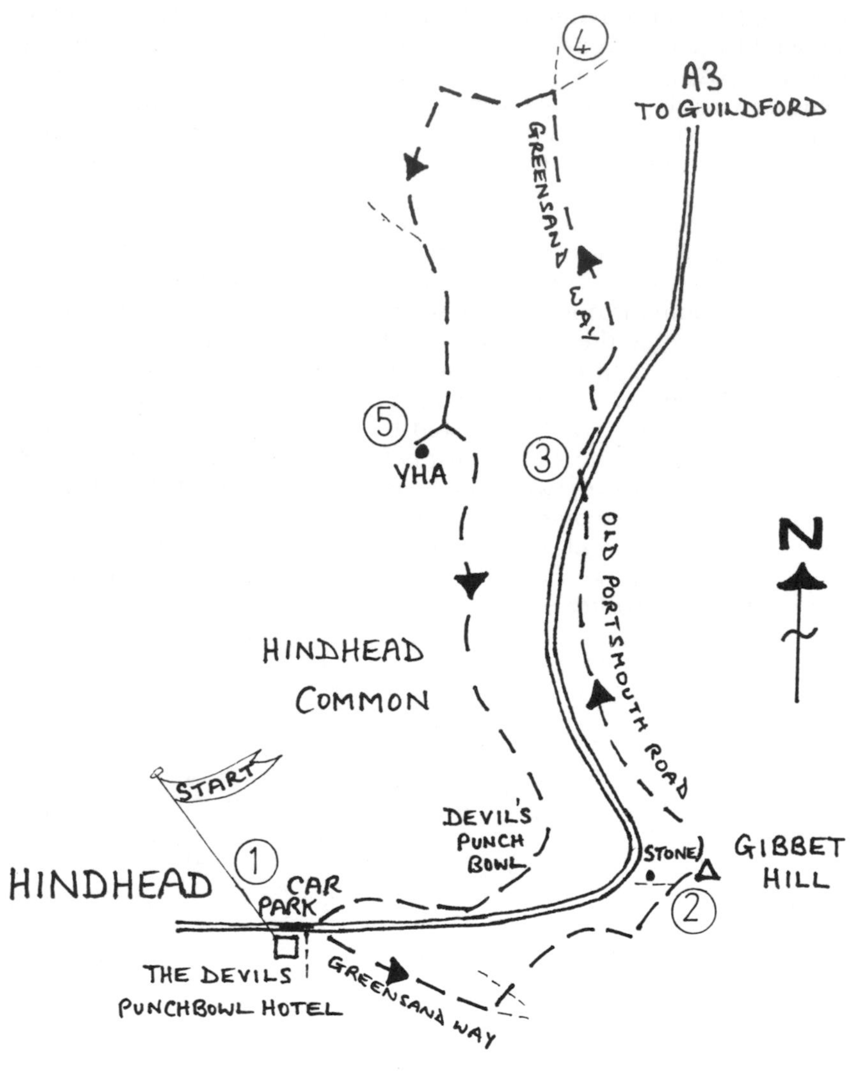

3 Bear right on a track which takes you under a metal barrier. In about 50 yards fork left on an uphill path (No Horses, No Cycles), taking you to a viewpoint with a seat. Continue on down the other side of the hillock and rejoin the track you left earlier. You pass a gate/stile and a seat on your left. Ignore another turning on the left and continue downhill to a crossing track.

4 Turn left, thus leaving the Greensand Way, and shortly your track is joined by another coming in from the right. Continue on between gates and pass a memorial seat on your left and a turning on the right going down a slope. You pass an isolated homestead, Gnome Cottage, and go up a slope to a T-junction by a spring. Turn right for 100 yards to see the youth hostel, a former broom maker's cottage, famed for its isolation.

5 Retrace your steps to the spring and continue forward, passing a pair of cottages on your right. Continue ahead on a tarred, uphill track for about 100 yards, where you bear right at a fork. The views over Hindhead Common open out as your path undulates and reaches a right turn by some fire beaters. Do not take the inviting grassy track ahead, but turn right on the stony one. You now commence your ascent to the rim of the Devil's Punch Bowl and your path becomes more narrow. Later you are assisted by some steps with a handrail, taking you towards the A3 but, just before reaching it, you turn right on a level path, passing two more seats. Pass a downward turning on the right and a couple branching off to the left as you continue around the contour of the hill and reach some wide steps. Turn left and shortly walk across the car park by the Hillcrest Café to reach the A3 and the hotel opposite.

16 Holmbury St Mary
The Kings Head

The Kings Head (freehouse) has been a pub since 1835, the old brewhouse having now been converted into a games room. The interior is particularly welcoming, with hops hanging from the beams and a cosy log fire in winter. There are some interesting photographs of the pub through the past century or so. Also on the wall is a fascinating showcase with eight miniature cricket bats, illustrating how their shape has changed since the game started in the 1720s. They include W.G. Grace's bat from the beginning of this century and the one used from the 1930s to this day.

The landlady takes charge of the food and almost all is home made by a French chef. There are Sunday roasts in the winter and the specials on the board, which are changed regularly, will include such dishes as pheasant or venison casserole when in season. For smaller appetites there are the usual sandwiches and ploughman's. Real ale buffs come from far and wide to savour the marvellous range of hand-pumped beers, most of which are best tasted *after* your walk rather than before. These include Ringwood, Brakspear, Badger, London Pride, the extremely potent Old Thumper plus guest beers. The draught cider is Scrumpy Jack. There is a dining area behind the bar where children can sit and a garden for them at the rear, with swings and climbing frames. Well-behaved dogs are also welcome. As a service to the local community, there is a small shop attached to and run by the pub. This must be the only place in Surrey to gain a village store instead of losing one during the past decade.

The opening hours are Monday to Friday 11 am–3 pm and 6 pm–11 pm, Saturday 11 am–11 pm, and Sunday 12 noon–3 pm and 7 pm–10.30 pm. Food is served on Monday to Saturday 12 noon–2.30 pm and 6.45 pm–9.15 pm, and on Sunday 12 noon–2.30 pm only.

Telephone: 0306 730282.

How to get there: Leave the A25 at Abinger Hammer and take the B2126, signposted to Holmbury St Mary, 3 miles or so south. About 200 yards beyond the church, turn right and shortly find the pub on your left.

Parking: Although space in front of the pub is limited, you are welcome to use it whilst on your walk if you ask permission. Otherwise, with due consideration for others, park along the road as there is really no alternative.

Length of the walk: 3 miles. OS maps: Landranger 187 or Pathfinder 1226 (GR 112442).

Much of the walk is on well-defined forest tracks, the highlight being the wonderful panoramic view from Holmbury Hill. The beautifully crafted toposcope adds to the pleasure as you pick out landmarks from 2 to 20 or more miles away.

The Walk

1 From the pub cross over and take the road which climbs left uphill. When you reach another road bear right and shortly turn sharp right on a public footpath shown as part of the Greensand Way and the way to Holmbury St Mary Cricket Club. The stony track bears left uphill and later you pass the cricket ground with its pavilion over on your right. The track forks and you keep left, still following the Greensand Way. You reach the open area of Somerset Hill and a junction of several paths.

2 Turn left on the bridleway and Greensand Way. You reach a fork and bear right, shortly going up a slope which gradually takes you up Holmbury Hill where you will enjoy excellent views over on your left. The South Downs are on the skyline and Leith Hill is to your left. At the next fork keep left, along the escarpment of the hill. Stay on the main track, still following the Greensand Way markers, and eventually

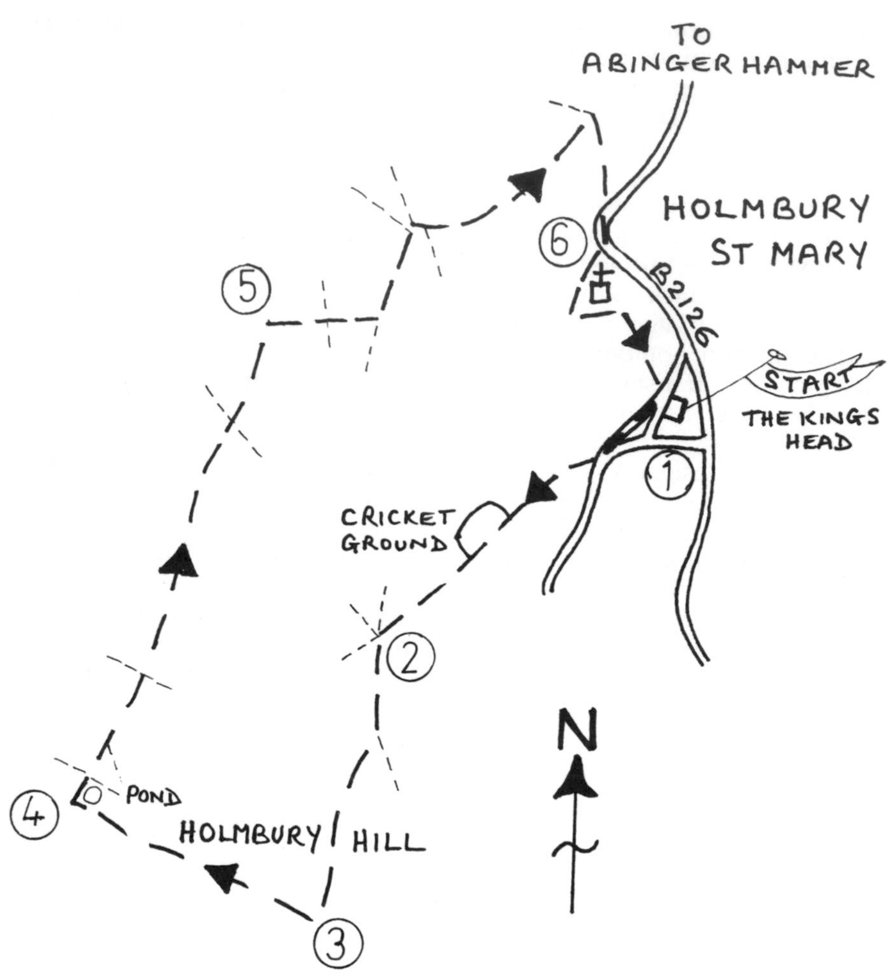

emerge at the top of Holmbury Hill, with its attractive circular seat and excellent toposcope, which shows the pattern of field and woodland as well as the distant hills. At 857 ft above sea level, this is Surrey's fourth highest summit and is the site of an Iron Age camp.

3 Rest awhile and take in the excellent views of several of Surrey's best-loved hills, and much beyond. With your back to the views walk a few yards to a Greensand Way marker on a post and bear left down a slope. Soon ignore a right fork and pass a metal seat on your left, dedicated to two young mountain climbers. At the next fork keep left, then left again at the following one, still following the Greensand Way.

Keep left yet again, still on the contour of the hill, and reach a clearing with a pond on your right.

4 Turn right, passing the pond on your right, and soon go over a crossing track. Maintain direction on a wide forestry road and shortly another track joins from the right. Continue on for about ¾ mile, going over two crossing tracks on the way.

5 Shortly after the second crossing track, fork right uphill. At the top of the slope go over a crossing track, then reach a wide crossing track onto which you turn left. In about 200 yards the main track bears left to a crossing track onto which you turn right. Ignore an immediate right turn and later go under cables to reach a T-junction with an orange marker pointing left. You turn right and shortly reach a fork, keeping left on a small path which takes you downhill to a road.

6 Cross the road and turn right, passing the green at Holmbury St Mary. Re-cross the road and join a tarred driveway to the church, which was designed and given to the village in 1879 by George Edward Street, the architect of the Law Courts in London, who settled at Holmdale. Opposite a garage turn left on a narrow path under trees which will shortly take you, via a gate, into the churchyard. Immediately fork right to continue on the raised path to the right of the church, passing some steps and a seat. Leave the churchyard via another gate and your narrow path then continues behind houses and above the village. It eventually brings you down to a lane on which you bear right, back to the pub.

17 Limpsfield Chart
The Carpenters Arms

The Carpenters Arms (Ind Coope), or 'The Chippies' as it is affectionately known, is a 'local' in the truest sense. All the old traditional pub games are played here, darts, dominoes, crib – even shove-ha'penny. The pub goes back about 200 years, the woodworking connection being that part of the building was once a sawpit. The management are enthusiastic and the atmosphere friendly.

The food is good, as well. If you are really hungry, order one of the home-made 'original country pies' – and there are five to choose from. The menu is extensive, much of the food being home cooked, and you can have anything from a bowl of soup (served with crusty bread from a local, traditional baker) to a sirloin steak. There are also two or three daily specials on the blackboard. Vegetarians have at least three choices, too. Friary, Tetley and Burton are the real ales on offer and Olde English cider and Guinness also come via pumps. Besides a bar full of memorabilia, there is a restaurant area where children are welcome – but no dogs, please. Outside there are two beer gardens – the larger one with a play area for the little ones.

The opening hours are Monday to Saturday 11 am–2.30 pm and 6 pm–11 pm, Sunday 12 noon–3 pm and 7 pm–10.30 pm. Food is served on Monday to Saturday 12 noon–2 pm and 7 pm–9 pm, and on Sunday 12 noon–2 pm only.

Telephone: 0883 722209.

How to get there: From the A25 at Limpsfield, east of Redhill, take the B269 going south-east. In 1½ miles fork left into Tally Road. The pub is on the left.

Parking: The pub has a car park which you are welcome to use whilst on the walk, but please let someone know. If this is full, there is plenty of room on the road outside plus a small parking area opposite.

Length of the walk: 5 miles. OS maps: Landranger 187 or Pathfinder 1208 (GR 425418).

Although there are no steep slopes for you to climb, you will certainly have some fine views across the Weald and also towards the North Downs skyline. This area is very close to the Kent border and has some of the characteristics of that county. A former oast house is passed and also some white weatherboarding is in evidence.

The Walk

1 From the pub turn left down the road with the village green on your right. Cross over a road to the path opposite taking you onto the Greensand Way and you will see St Andrew's church over on your right. In a few yards, just before a notice directed at horse riders, bear left onto a wide, grassy path. Ignore a right fork and other branching paths and eventually reach a yellow waymark where you bear right, joining a path coming in from the left. Go over a crossing track and take a left fork onto the yellow-waymarked footpath. At the next fork go right, passing a large Scots pine on your right (there is a small yellow arrow on a tree), and this path will bring you down past a pond.

2 Continue ahead, crossing a track and passing a seat, taking the narrow path on your left and go along the edge of a young plantation. You are now in The High Chart, which is actively managed by the Forestry Authority. Later, pass a waymarked post and continue on this narrow path. Another path comes in from the left by a waymark and you continue forward. Later, arrive at a T-junction where you turn left for a few yards towards a gate and road, but before reaching them turn right onto a narrow path. In about 200 yards or so you come to a crossing track by a waymark and turn left onto this meandering path through bracken. In about 250 yards you meet a gravelled path on which you turn left to the road, crossing it with care.

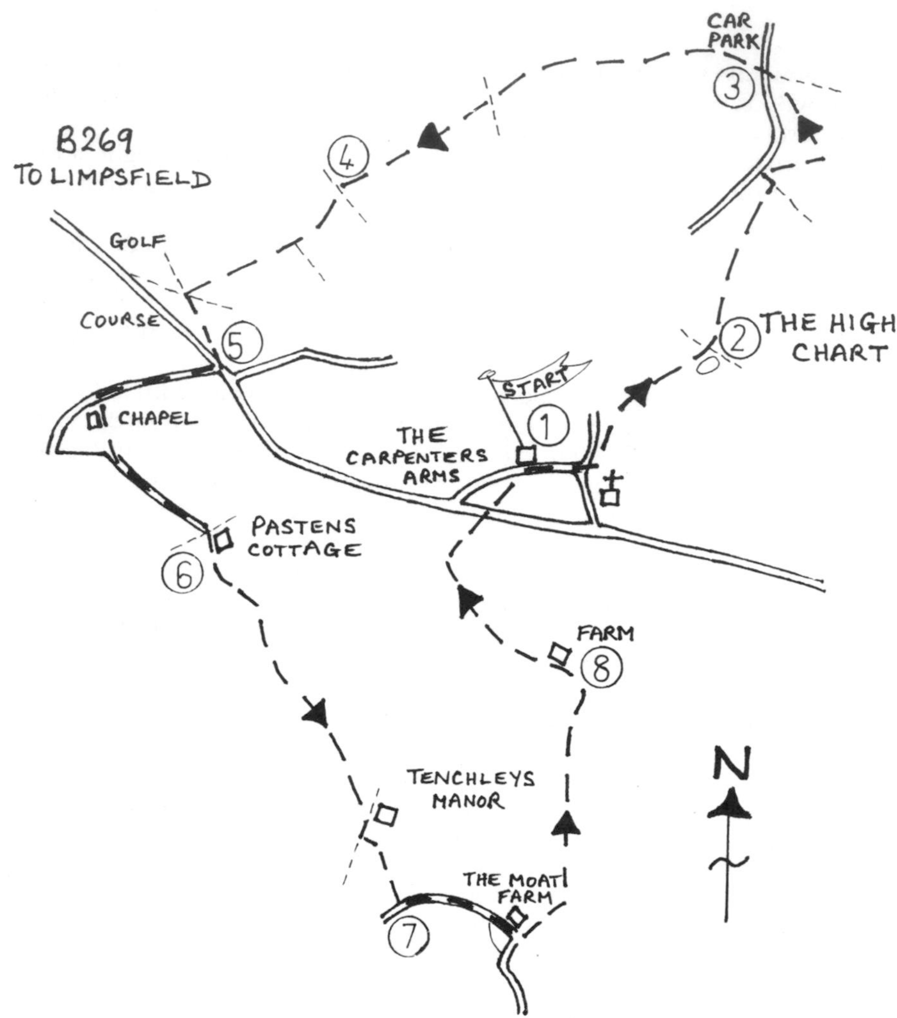

3 Go through a car park serving a recreation ground over on the right, and through two short, wooden posts to continue on a path with a beech-lined boundary bank on your left. Your path dips to an area of fallen trees and you bear right. Ignore a right fork and remain on the wider, sandy path on the left with an open area on your left. Pass a waymark and continue with a field on your right, going through a bridle gate. Head straight across a field to another gate and back into woods with fields over on your right. Go over a crossing track by a gate and waymark, continuing with more fields over on your right. Later, ignore a turning on the left but in a few more yards, just after a waymark, turn left and shortly go over a plank bridge and stile.

Continue over the narrow end of a field, over a farm track and back into woods. You come out into another field which you cross towards a gateway, but do not go through.

4 Turn left along the field edge, following a hedge on your right, and in the corner cross a stile back into more woods. Ignore a turning on the left. Another track comes in from the left and you continue forward towards a golf course. Make your way along the right-hand side of a fairway and, at the end of this, go down a dip and take the second of the two turnings on the left. Shortly, go over another fairway and your path bears round to the left where you meet a T-junction and turn right towards a road junction.

5 Turn right across the road and take the road opposite with another part of the golf course over on your right. In about 300 yards, just before the road curves left, turn left over a stile by a chapel and back onto the Greensand Way for a short distance. Continue on an enclosed path and later go through a kissing gate and out to a residential road by a former oast house. Turn left and, if the conditions are clear, you should enjoy good views over to the North Downs on your right. At the end of the road you reach a four-way fingerpost with Pastens Cottage on your left, the home, in exile, of the 19th century Russian writer Sergey Kravehensky Stephniak.

6 Leaving the Greensand Way once again, continue straight ahead on a driveway but, just before reaching a house, turn left through a gate in the fence and then turn right on an enclosed path which soon becomes tunnel-like. Your path goes downhill to a stile which you cross into a field. Continue down the right-hand side of the field, with a gully down on your right, enjoying excellent views in front of you across the Weald. At the bottom go over a stile and continue along an enclosed path, pass some grain silos and reach the driveway to Tenchleys Manor which you will see over on your left. Bear right, past a pond and a pair of wooden posts, and bear left off the drive to cross a footbridge into a field. Turn right, across the field, and make for a stile by a gate, taking you out to a road.

7 Turn left along the road which later curves right, past an attractive duck-pond opposite The Moat Farm. This was originally a 15th century hallhouse and traces of the site of the moat may be detected. By the entrance to The Old Lodge, turn left over a stile with a fingerpost. Turn left along the edge of a field and make for a stile in the hedge ahead. Continue along the left edge of the next field and go over another stile and straight across the next field. Go through a farm gate and turn right along a grassy farm track which later curves to the left, and then commence a gentle climb to another gate leading you into Chartlands Farm.

8 Join a driveway and continue uphill, soon enjoying excellent views over the fence on your left. Continue ahead on a roadway, passing a large house, Caxton House, on your right. Pass the driveway to Spring Cottage and turn right onto a footpath by a three-way fingerpost. There is a stone wall on your right. Go straight across a drive and continue up a slope, passing two houses on your right, and then join a grassy track curving round to the right. You come out to another drive to a house and turn left along this. The driveway curves to the left and brings you out to a road which you cross with care. Head across the green, back to the pub.

18 Little London
The William IV

The William IV (freehouse) is a real, family-run country pub with no pretensions and no desire to move into the 21st century. Many of the locals, who are prepared to share this gem of a pub with you, still refer to it by its former name, The Garibaldi, especially the real old 'uns whose memories go back to the 1914–18 War. Once a farmhouse, most of the building dates from 1578. Later the local gentry gave permission for its change to an alehouse, where the workers from the fields could drown their sorrows and temporarily forget their miserable lot.

Food here is first-rate, the best meat being brought home from Smithfield and fish from Billingsgate. Specialities of the house are pheasant, hare and venison when in season. If you should happen to time your visit to the third Saturday in the month, spit-roast venison, pork or lamb is on offer. On the first Saturday there is fresh seafood. Round off your meal with one of the delicious, traditional puddings. Although the food is special, the prices are not and represent excellent value for money. People come from far and wide to enjoy the Sunday roasts and vegetarians will not go hungry either. The list of real ales is impressive, and is frequently changed, five or six always being available. The regular ciders are Strongbow and Merrydown. There is no problem with children or dogs and the atmosphere is very relaxed.

The opening hours are Monday to Saturday 11 am–3 pm and 5.30 pm–11 pm, Sunday 12 noon–3 pm and 7 pm–10.30 pm. Food is served on Monday to Saturday 12 noon–2.30 pm and 7 pm–10 pm, and on Sunday 12 noon–2.30 pm and 7.30 pm–9.30 pm.

Telephone: 0483 202685.

How to get there: Little London is well hidden away but may be found south of the A25 by taking the turning for Shere. From Shere go south on Sandy Lane and, just before a railway bridge, take the right turn, signposted to Albury. Alternatively, you may reach it from the A248 east of Albury. At a sharp turn, take New Road and, in less than a mile, turn left into Park Road. Take the second turning on the right, into Little London. From either direction you will find the pub on your right.

Parking: The pub has an adequate car park which you may use, with permission, whilst you take the walk. If the car park is full it is possible to park on the road outside the pub, but please consider local residents.

Length of the walk: 3¾ miles. OS maps: Landranger 187 or Pathfinder 1226 (GR 066467).

There are no steep hills, only gentle slopes and many pleasant views. Although close to one of Surrey's best-loved towns, Guildford, you are in the heart of the countryside and remote from civilisation on most of this walk. Farmland and woodland will be found in equal measure on this tranquil route.

The Walk

1 From the pub turn right down the road, taking a footpath on the right just before the railway bridge. You go up this fenced path, later ignoring a gate on the left, through a barrier and onto Albury Heath. Bear right onto a track and pass a small red-brick building on the right. Go over a crossing track and bear left, taking the wider of the two tracks on the left. Go over the next crossing track, pass a turning on the right and continue to a road. Cross straight over and in a few yards reach a crossing track. Turn right and shortly reach a recreation ground. Continue along the right-hand side of this, keeping parallel with the road. On the right, notice the plaque commemorating Monty's visit here in 1944. Shortly you reach a parking area.

2 Bear right onto a waymarked path which then bears left, downhill. Via barriers you go over a crossing track and up a slope. Another path

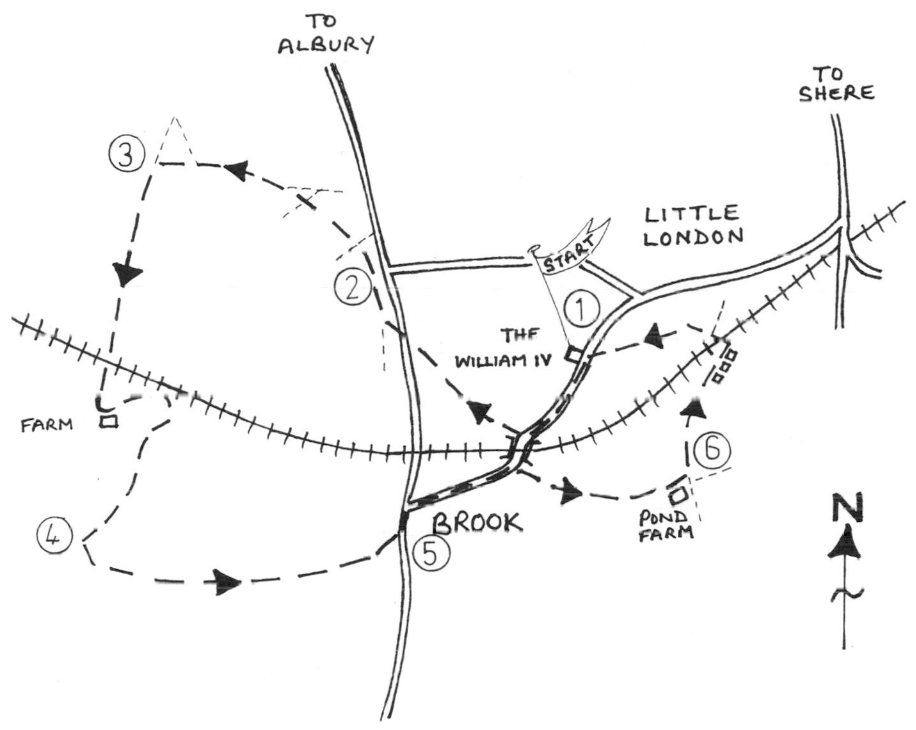

comes in from the right and you continue ahead. Go over a crossing track and reach an open area. The building on the left, with the distinctive Pugin-designed chimneys that are a feature of the area, was once the village school. Pass through a gate leading you onto a public bridleway going through Albury Warren. Later ignore a branching bridleway to the right and continue ahead for another 200 yards to reach a crossing footpath where there are two redundant stiles.

3 Turn left onto the public footpath and go through a plantation, at the end of which you go over a stile and into a field. Here you turn left towards two or three large trees, following an easily identifiable path. Over to your right is St Martha's church on the top of the hill. At the bottom of the field cross a railway line with care and continue forward to a tree-lined, sunken path. Go through a metal gate and bear left to an attractive, timbered farmhouse. Go through another gate and turn left between farm buildings. You pass some sadly neglected watercress beds on your right and come out to a T-junction. Turn right on another bridleway, going over a bridge. Your sandy track goes gradually uphill for about ⅓ mile where you reach a fork.

4 Bear left on a footpath and, at the next fork, keep left again. In a few more yards you reach a crossing track and turn left along this wide, grassy track through a plantation. Eventually cross a stile, and go across a field down and over another stile. Maintain direction along the perimeter of the next field, reaching a fingerpost where you bear slightly left down a track and come out to a road in the hamlet of Brook.

5 Turn left along the road and then turn right into Brook Lane, passing some charming cottages. Look particularly for Chennels, built in 1636, with curious wood carvings on the roof timbers. You keep along this lane, heading towards the railway bridge which you passed earlier in the walk. Just before reaching it, take the farm driveway on the right, signposted as a footpath, and continue along it until you reach Ponds Farm. You go over a stile by a gate leading you onto an enclosed path and then cross another stile bringing you out to a T-junction.

6 Turn left and continue along another sandy bridleway which eventually merges with a tarred track and passes a row of houses on your right. You come to a gate leading to the railway which you again cross with care. Go ahead on a path, ignoring an immediate right turn. In about 200 yards reach a turning on the left which you take, ignoring an immediate left fork. Continue on this narrow path which goes into a shallow gully and brings you out to the road opposite the pub.

19 Mickleham
The King William IV

The King William IV (freehouse) is part Victorian but principally dates from 1790. Later it became an alehouse for the estate workers of the local landowner, Lord Beaverbrook. The pub has an unusually attractive setting and is perched on a hillside with a flight of steps for access. The bars are quite small and, consequently, cosy.

The chef happens to be the proprietor and a good selection of innovative dishes are always available as well as the usual pub snacks. These include fish and vegetarian dishes, all of which are cooked on the premises. Traditional roasts are served on Sundays. Only well-kept, real ales are served and these include Boddingtons, Adnams and Badger plus a guest beer. Neither children nor dogs are allowed in the bar, but there is an attractive, terraced garden, where on good summer days barbecues are held.

The opening hours are Monday to Saturday 11 am–3 pm and 6 pm–11 pm, Sunday 12 noon–3 pm and 7 pm–10.30 pm. Food is served on Monday to Saturday 12 noon–2.15 pm, Tuesday to Saturday 7 pm–9 pm, and on Sunday 12 noon–2.15 pm only.

Telephone: 0372 372590.

How to get there: The pub is situated in a lane, Byttom Hill, which is just off the A24 (Leatherhead–Dorking road), behind the Frascati restaurant. If travelling south, leave the A24 just before the Mickleham sign and if travelling north, immediately after it.

Parking: The pub does not have a car park so you should park considerately in Byttom Hill or in the lane leading off to a school, ensuring that residents' entrances are not blocked. It is also possible to park on the A24 alongside the houses or, better still, on the grass verge on the opposite side.

Length of the walk: 3¾ miles. OS maps: Landranger 187 or Pathfinder 1206 (GR 174538).

This beautiful walk, which includes one climb, takes you over Mickleham Downs and along a stretch of grassland known as White Hill. Sometimes you will feel you are on south-east England's roof as, on a clear day, the views across London and beyond are magnificent. Autumn is a particularly good time for this walk, when the brilliant colours of the foliage will be especially striking here. Be warned – the chalky slopes will be slippery after rain.

The Walk

1 From the pub return towards the main road, Mickleham Bypass, but before reaching it turn left on a rough track passing houses and later a school on your left. Your path narrows as you pass a children's

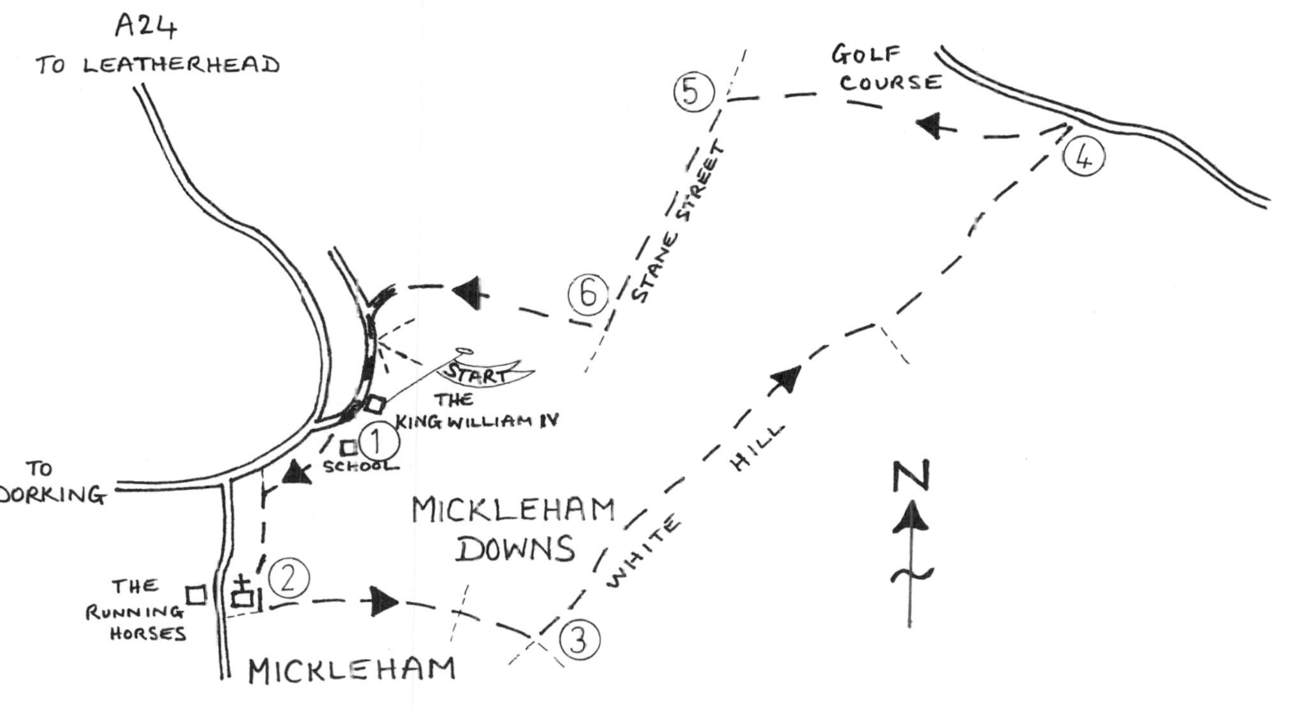
A24
TO LEATHERHEAD
GOLF COURSE
STANE STREET
START
THE KING WILLIAM IV
SCHOOL
TO DORKING
MICKLEHAM DOWNS
WHITE HILL
N
THE RUNNING HORSES
MICKLEHAM
1
2
3
4
5
6

recreation ground on the left and on reaching a T-junction you turn left. Go over a tarred driveway and continue ahead through the churchyard, with St Michael's church, where the novelist Fanny Burney was married, on your right. Leave via a gate onto a track. There is a public house, The Running Horses, on the other side of the church, with an interesting sign depicting the dead heat Derby finish of 1828.

2 Turn left and shortly cross a stile to the right of some white gates. Continue uphill on an enclosed path which starts to become more steep. Eventually you go over a crossing track, with a National Trust sign for Mickleham Downs on your left, and continue to a wooden post waymarked 'NT Long Walk' with a figure '6'.

3 Turn left onto a meandering path, taking you under trees and shortly emerge onto an area where trees have obviously been removed. Pass another National Trust post and bear right onto the open area of White Hill, a well-documented habitat of many varieties of butterfly and moth. Keep to the right of a row of posts holding a single length of wire, as horse riders are likely to come charging along this lovely straight ride. You should have good views over to your left and occasionally on the right. Where the ride ends, go under the wire and continue on the enclosed track ahead, ignoring the direction of the next National Trust post on the right. Go past a green gate on your right and keep to the track for about ½ mile where, just before a road, you will find another signposted bridleway on your left.

4 Turn sharply left onto the bridleway and shortly you will find an attractive golf course on your right, with excellent views beyond. In about another ½ mile, go over a crossing track and continue for a few yards to another.

5 Turn left on the red-waymarked bridleway forming part of the old Roman road, Stane Street, which at one time would have taken you from London to Chichester. Continue on this undulating track for almost another ½ mile where you should look out on your right for an easily missed yellow waymark on a fallen tree.

6 Turn right on the narrow footpath and follow this and the wire fence on your left. After going through a tunnel of trees you are taken down some steps to a tarred lane leading to a house on the right. Turn left on the lane and shortly join another on which you bear left, going slightly uphill. Very shortly you reach a junction of several tracks and take the one on the far right, going downhill, which in a few minutes will bring you back to the pub.

20 Mogador
The Sportsman

The Sportsman (Courage) is so tucked away on the edge of Walton Heath that, unless a local, you are unlikely to have found it other than by recommendation. It dates back to the 1500s when it was used as a hunting lodge by members of the Royal Family, hence the sporting connection. It is documented as a place for drinking as far back as 1737. At that time it catered for drovers and horse riders from the surrounding heathland and would have been a haunt of smugglers, particularly those evading the coal and wine tolls. Toll posts survive in the vicinity to this day. Nowadays it is popular with walkers who, on weekdays, mingle with office workers briefly escaping their concrete towers.

The food is varied, much of it being home cooked. Besides the regular menu, the blackboard tempts you with other delights, but hurry with your order as these dishes are popular and may disappear from the board even whilst you read. If you would like morning coffee and cakes before your walk these are available daily from 10 am. Real ale lovers will find Wadworth 6X, Courage Best and Directors. Try the guest ale if you want something different. Cider drinkers have a choice of Dry Blackthorn or Red Rock. Children may

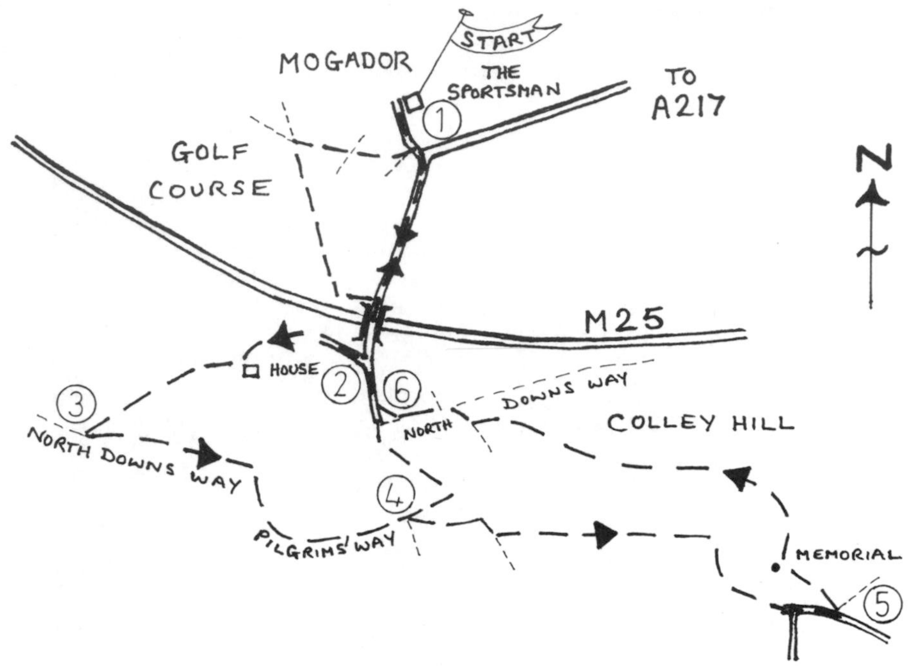

come inside and so may dogs, as long as they are not too muddy. For fine days there is a large garden with equipment to keep the kids amused.

The opening hours are Monday to Saturday 11 am–3 pm and 5.30 pm–11 pm, Sunday 12 noon–3 pm and 7 pm–10.30 pm. Food is served every day 12 noon–2.30 pm and 7 pm–10 pm.

Telephone: 0737 246655.

How to get there: Mogador lies between Banstead and Reigate. From junction 8 of the M25, go north on the A217 (Brighton Road). In ½ mile, at a roundabout, turn left on Stubbs Lane, which goes over a crossroads to Mogador Road. At the end of this, turn right to the pub (signposted).

Parking: The pub has a very large car park which you may use, with permission, whilst on your walk.

Length of the walk: 4½ miles, or 3½ miles if you wish to avoid a steep slope, which will be slippery after rain. OS maps: Landranger 187 or Pathfinder 1207 (GR 240531).

This walk promises some great views, particularly from Colley Hill towards the end. You will want to allow time to linger over them. After crossing over the speeding traffic of the M25 you will be led to pleasant woodland paths where you can imagine more tranquil times in the past.

The Walk

1 From the pub turn left, back down the road, and, just before reaching a junction, turn right on a tarred public bridleway. (If there has been a considerable amount of rain and you want to avoid muddy tracks further on, do not turn right onto the bridleway. Instead, continue to the junction and turn right on the road. You will cross the M25 and reach a turning on the right at point 2.)

Ignore a turning on the left and go over a crossing track, shortly reaching another by a coal and wine post, where tolls would have been levied, up until 1889, on goods being taken into London. Turn left, soon passing another coal post and, very shortly, yet another. The world-famous Walton Heath Golf Course is over on your right and very soon the roar of the traffic on the M25 will become apparent. Later the path curves left alongside the motorway and you reach a bridge taking you across it. Continue for about a 100 yards or so to a turning on the right.

2 *For the longer route, which includes a steep, downhill slope:* Turn right on the road and, immediately after passing through the posts leading into a private housing estate, turn left on the drive to Conybury Heights. Just to the right of some wooden gates, go over a stile onto a narrow, enclosed path. Now be prepared for a steep slope which will be slippery after rain, but where there are plenty of trees and shrubs which you can use to steady yourself as you make your descent. At the bottom go down some steps to a crossing track.

For the shorter route, avoiding a steep, downhill slope: Do not turn right but continue to the end of the road and bear left past a coal post, onto the North Downs Way. The downhill track swings left and later right, bringing you to a crossing track with wooden barriers at point 4 where you turn left.

3 Turn left onto the North Downs Way. You should now be enjoying good views. The path curves to the right and you are sheltered as you walk under a pleasant canopy of trees, eventually passing through a wooden barrier.

4 Go over a crossing track, continuing through a barrier and leave the North Downs Way. The path you are on is part of the Pilgrims' Way and shaded by an impressive forest of yew trees. Shortly, pass a turning on the right and continue on your track, which soon bears to the right. On reaching a fork, bear right down some steps, aided by a handrail. Ignore a couple of turnings on the left and a right fork. A large house and farm buildings come into view. Go through a barrier by a gate and onto a road, continuing on this to the point where it commences to slope downwards.

5 Bear left and then turn left through two white, metal posts and follow the high, brick wall on your right. Later this chalky path becomes more steep but you are helped by some occasional steps. Pass the granite memorial to Captain George Simpson and shortly find metal railings on your left. Later you pass an old wooden seat on your right and very shortly you are led onto the grassy, open space of Colley Hill. When you reach the next seat bear left, passing another seat on your immediate right. Soon after you pass the next, dilapidated seat, fork right up a slope and go through an 'arch' in the hedgerow ahead. Continue along the escarpment of the hill, passing an ornate water tower over to your right, and eventually you will reach a point where the path slopes steeply downhill. Here you should bear right to find a path running through shrubs, still following the contour of the hill. You reach a T-junction and turn right to go through a squeeze stile, passing a sign for Colley Hill. At another T-junction, turn left, back onto the North Downs Way, soon ignoring a turning on the right. Pass a coal post and, at a fork by a barrier, continue right, shortly going through some posts and out to the minor road you were on near the beginning of the walk.

6 Turn right along the road and remain on it for about ⅓ mile, passing a left turning and going back over the M25 motorway. Ignore all turnings and you will reach the road junction by 'The Sportsman' sign, where you turn left, back to the pub.

21 Newlands Corner
The Manor

The Manor (freehouse) is a hotel but has a bar patronised by locals and visitors to the nearby Newlands Corner viewpoint. At 500 ft above sea level it has good views over five counties. Before becoming a hotel in the 1920s, it started life as a country house, built in the 1890s by Lytton Strachey who went on to form the famous 'Bloomsbury Group'. Many are said to have experienced the presence of spirits from this period. The welcoming panelled bar, which has a separate entrance, is thickly carpeted and has a roaring log-effect fire in winter.

On offer is food of the quality one should expect from a smart hotel's kitchen. The menu covers every requirement of the hungry walker, from sandwiches, freshly baked, filled rolls and soups to more exotic dishes. If you enjoy a ploughman's you may want to try 'The Manor Ploughmans' which includes a selection of cheeses and cold meats. Complementing the regular menu are the 'chef specials' on the blackboard, all reasonably priced. All the food is prepared and cooked on the premises, including the desserts. If you have room for it, try one of the puddings, together with some delicious home-made ice-cream. There are usually two real ales available, Fuller's London Pride being the regular one. Cider is only served from bottles but Guinness is on tap. Supervised children are welcome in the bar, but dogs are not allowed. There is, however, a beer garden where they may sit with you, weather permitting.

The opening hours are Monday to Saturday 12 noon–2.30 pm and 6 pm–11 pm, Sunday 12 noon–3 pm and 7 pm–10.30 pm. Food is served every day 12 noon–2 pm and 7 pm–9.30 pm.

Telephone: 0483 222624.

How to get there: From the traffic lights at the junction of the A247, A246 and A25 near West Clandon, just east of Guildford, go uphill on the A25 Dorking road. In about ½ mile, towards the top of the slope and before an indicated right turn, the driveway to the hotel will be found on the left.

Parking: The hotel has plenty of parking which you are welcome to use whilst on the walk, but please let the staff know. If you would prefer not to walk along the narrow verge by the busy A25 to commence and conclude the walk you should park at the nearby Newlands Corner car park and drive the short distance to the hotel afterwards.

Length of the walk: 3½ miles. OS maps: Landranger 186 or Pathfinder 1226 (GR 046497).

Newlands Corner has always been a popular viewpoint. On a clear day you can see Chanctonbury Ring on the South Downs. A whole range of hills are visible, from Reigate and Leith Hills in the east to Blackdown and Hindhead in the west. Although the car park is mostly jam-packed with people and cars, on the walk you will soon discover some quiet paths and probably have the countryside all to yourself.

The Walk

1 *If you are starting from the hotel:* Return down the driveway to the main road and turn left. Pass Carlo's Restaurant and cross the road with care. Continue along the grassy verge for a few yards and opposite Newlands House turn right on a footpath and pass a wooden barrier. There is a small brick building on your right and you continue through the woods for a couple of hundred yards to reach a road. Cross over and take the right-hand one of two paths. Shortly another path comes in from the left.

If you are starting from the public car park: Facing the information/refreshment centre take the concrete path on the right and continue ahead, shortly passing public toilets on your left. Continue on a well-defined track, soon passing a 'stag' waymark post. A small path comes in from the right and you go over a minor crossing track, shortly meeting a main track coming in from the right.

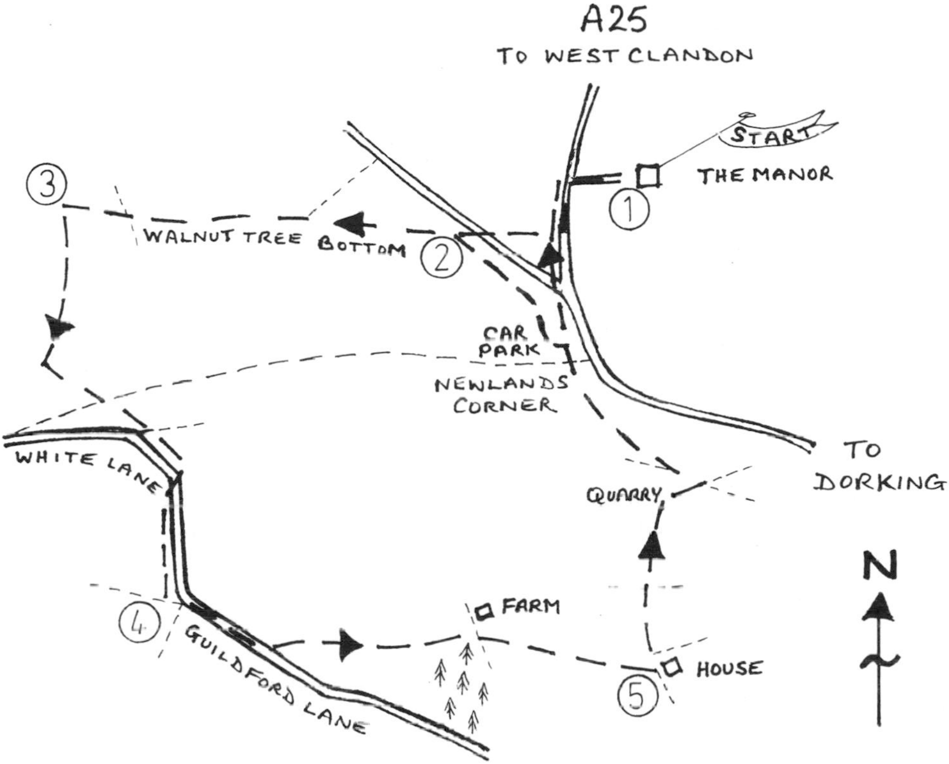

2 Continue ahead, ignoring turnings on the left and right and remaining on this path, known as Walnut Tree Bottom, for over ½ mile, passing a signposted footpath on the right about halfway along. Go over a crossing track and, about 200 yards further on, reach a wide, uphill turning on the left. There is a stone wall around a garden ahead.

3 Turn left uphill on this permissive horse ride, which eventually levels out. You reach a crossing bridleway where you continue ahead, going over a crossing footpath and a small car park named 'White Lane'. Continue on the horse ride, which is now quite narrow. Ignore a left fork but when you reach a post with a bovine sign, turn right. At the next post fork left, then go right through a barrier and out to a road. Cross over to and go up some steps opposite, then turn left on the narrow path which forms part of the North Downs Way. The path runs parallel with the road and eventually you reach a fingerpost by a house and turn left onto the road.

4 Turn right up Guildford Lane and shortly pass an entrance to a car park for St Martha's on your right. In 100 yards or so turn left on a fenced path, forming part of the Pilgrims' Way, passing another 'bovine' sign. As you pass along the second field on your right, look out for some llamas. You should be enjoying good open views on your left and shortly there is a conifer wood on your right. You reach a crossing track and go through a gate ahead. Bear diagonally right, uphill, across a field to a metal farm gate and, after passing through this, turn left through a bridlegate. Continue on the enclosed path which later goes downhill to a tarred track near a house.

5 Turn left, ignoring an immediate right turn, now following a 'sheep' route. Go over a crossing farm track and continue on your sloping one. After passing a disused quarry area, bear right, still on the 'sheep' track. Your path becomes stony and slightly more steep and you reach a crossing track by an old pillbox. Turn left on this permissive horse ride, still following the 'sheep' sign. Ignore a left fork and continue uphill. Pass a 'butterfly' signpost on the left and, at the top of the slope, cross over the road leading to the Newlands Corner car park. If you have not parked here you should go into the car park anyway just to take in the marvellous views.

To return to the hotel continue on the grassy verge alongside the main road. Cross over a left turning. The grass verge is more narrow here, so take care and shortly you will see the hotel entrance over on your right.

22 Peaslake
The Hurtwood Inn

The Hurtwood Inn (freehouse) is an imposing sight in the centre of this sleepy village. However, do not feel intimidated by its 1920s grandeur, for besides being a smart hotel it also serves as the village local where everyone is welcome. If you are seeking comfortable accommodation near a good area for walking, look no further.

As this is a hotel, food is available at all times. There is always a comprehensive, mouth-watering selection of bar meals on the board, which includes daily specials prepared by the hotel chef. The curry dishes come very highly recommended. If you really want to splash out the restaurant cuisine is of the high standard you would expect of an elegant hotel. In the bar, real ale lovers may refresh themselves with either Courage Best, Wadworth 6X or the guest beer. If you are visiting in the afternoon, tea taken in the restful lounge or in the garden may be a more appropriate option. Children are welcome, as are well-behaved dogs.

The opening hours are Monday to Friday 11 am – 3 pm and 6 pm – 11 pm, Saturday 11 am – 11 pm and Sunday 12 noon – 3 pm and 7 pm – 10.30 pm. Food is served all the time.

Telephone: 0306 730851.

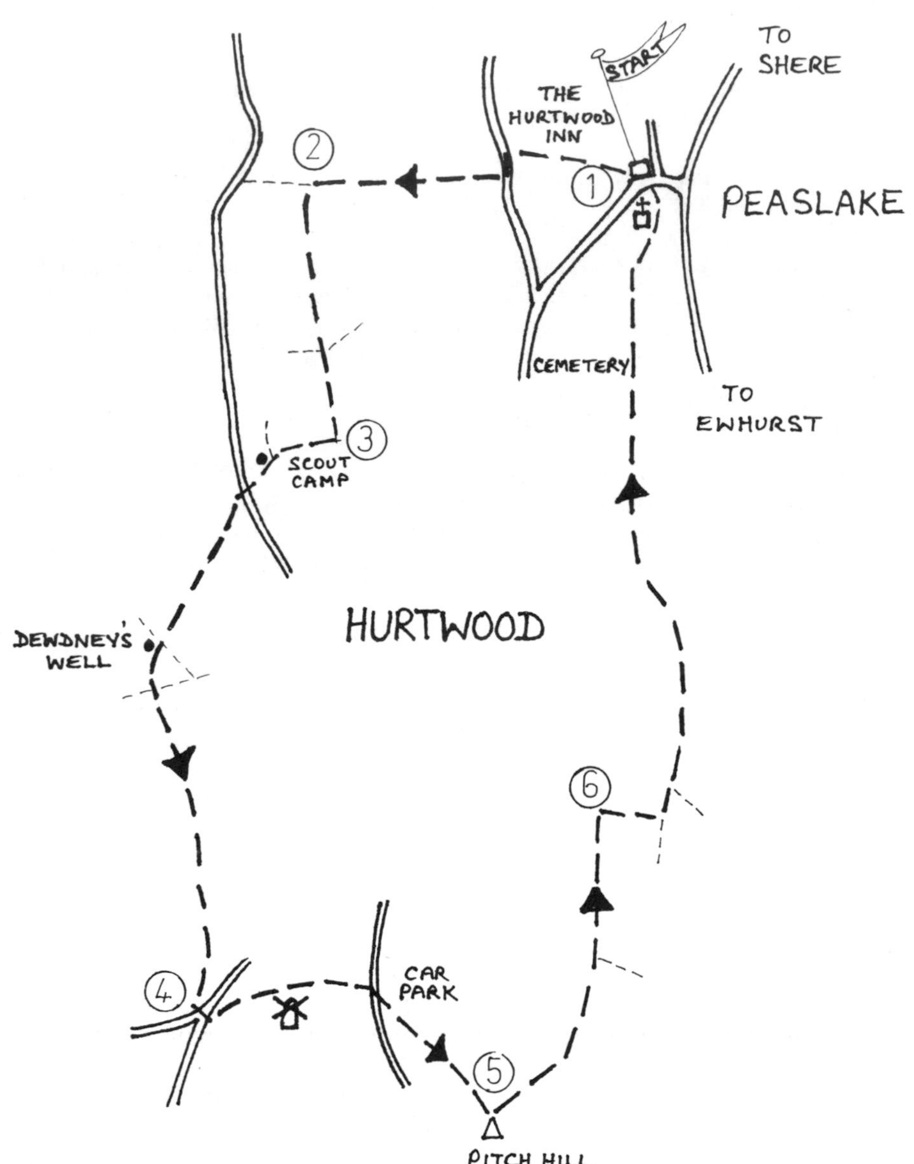

START
TO SHERE
THE HURTWOOD INN
PEASLAKE
CEMETERY
TO EWHURST
SCOUT CAMP
DEWDNEY'S WELL
HURTWOOD
CAR PARK
PITCH HILL
1
2
3
4
5
6

How to get there: Midway between Guildford and Dorking, leave the A25 for Shere and then take the Ewhurst road. After crossing a railway bridge, turn left and you will reach Peaslake 2 miles later. The inn is right in the centre of the village and cannot be missed.

Parking: You may park on the inn forecourt or in the road (no yellow lines). Behind the inn, off Pond Lane, is its own car park and just nearby there is a public one.

Length of the walk: 4¾ miles. OS maps: Landranger 187 or Pathfinder 1226 (GR 086447).

This most pleasant walk takes you over farmland and a large area of the woodland comprising the 4,000-acre Hurtwood Forest. A climb to the summit of Pitch Hill, Surrey's fifth highest, rewards you with sweeping views across the Weald and Sussex Downs beyond.

The Walk

1 From the inn's entrance turn right and leave the village by immediately bearing right up an enclosed footpath. Go ahead along a field edge and, ignoring a stile on the right, go down a drive to a road. Turn left for about 100 yards and then turn right on a track just before reaching The Parsonage. Go along the left side of a recreation ground, through a gate and then continue ahead along the right-hand side of a field and through a wicket gate.

2 Turn left across a field and go through a gate by a cottage. In just a few yards turn left off the track and immediately right, onto a path through a wood. In about 300 yards cross a boundary bank which marks the edge of the Hurtwood. Turn right downhill for a few yards and then turn left on a path with a bank on your right. Ignore turnings to the left and right and in about another 300 yards you will reach a wide crossing track.

3 Turn right, shortly passing Bentley Copse Scout Camp. Ignore a right turn and in about another 300 yards you will reach a road. Cross the road to the drive opposite and in a few yards bear left up a track. Follow the path as it goes up and then downhill to Dewdney's Well, hidden low in the trees. Go ahead over two crossing tracks and continue on a wide forest road. Keep ahead where the road bears left and ignore a turning to the right. In about 300 yards ignore a wide turning on the right and continue ahead to pass through a wicket gate where the bridleway narrows. Keep ahead for about another ⅓ mile and reach a road.

4 Turn left on the road and go straight ahead across another to a track opposite. Pass Summerfield Cottage and continue uphill, over a crossing track, for about 300 yards and reach a former windmill. From here bear left downhill on the Greensand Way. Follow a fence on your right and come down to a road. Cross the road to the Hurtwood Control car park 3. Cross the car park and then turn right on a sloping path, at first parallel to the road. Follow the path uphill and later, if you look to your left, you will see a huge sand quarry. The path starts to level out and you reach the triangulation point on the summit of Pitch Hill.

5 Continue ahead for about 50 yards then turn left on a path which runs round the hill. In about 200 yards pass a metal seat and shortly thereafter, where the Greensand Way dives down to the right, remain on the higher path. Keep ahead, going over a crossing track, and reach another. At the second crossing track you will have come to the end of mature, mixed woodland and the start of a fir tree plantation.

6 Turn right on the crossing track and, in about another 200 yards, reach a T-junction where you turn left, shortly passing a turning down to the right. Keep ahead on the broad track, ignoring all turnings, for a mile or so and eventually pass a cemetery on your left. At a fork bear right on a footpath leading past the church and out to the road opposite the inn.

23 Ranmore Common

The Ranmore Inn

The Ranmore Inn (freehouse) has only been a pub since the early 1970s although the building dates from earlier in the century when it was the Estate Manager's bungalow. It stands close to the Ranmore Manor which has recently been renovated. Being close to Ranmore Common, as well as the paths explored on our route, the pub has been a popular watering hole for walkers since it opened.

Good pub grub (the chips were really crunchy!) is available at down-to-earth prices. The regular menu is supplemented by daily specials and all the food is home cooked. On Sundays a traditional roast is served at 1 pm (order in good time) and in winter months a choice of two roasts is offered. To quench your thirst the range of real ales is impressive and includes Badger, London Pride, TEA, Tanglefoot, Pendragon, Tawny plus a guest beer and the ciders are Strongbow and Scrumpy Jack. Children are welcome and well-behaved dogs are allowed in the pub, but only in the evening (when food is not served). Outside is a patio area as well as a large garden where children may play and where barbecues take place in the summer. A limited amount of accommodation is also available in two chalets which each provide full facilities for one or two people.

The opening hours are Monday to Saturday 11 am–3 pm and 5.30 pm–11 pm, Sunday 12 noon–3 pm and 7 pm–10.30 pm. Food is served every day 12 noon–2.15 pm only.

Telephone: 0483 283783.

How to get there: The pub is off Ranmore Common Road, about 2 miles from East Horsley and 3 miles from Dorking. From East Horsley leave the A246 on Green Dene and fork left into Crocknorth Road which runs into Ranmore Common Road. From the A25 in Dorking take Station Road and fork left into Ranmore Road which runs into Ranmore Common Road. The pub's driveway is shared with Ranmore Manor and is a few yards east of the one to The Old Cartlodge Tea Rooms.

Parking: The pub has a car park and there is also an overflow area off the driveway. You are welcome to use the parking facilities but are asked to inform the staff that you are doing so.

Length of the walk: 5 miles. OS maps: Landranger 187 or Pathfinder 1206 and 1226 (GR 112502).

The walk commences on farmland and continues over an area of woodland. You use part of the North Downs Way where official changes to the defined route have been made to ensure that you get the best possible views. There may be mud after rain but you will often find a convenient, well-trodden, alternative path alongside the main tracks.

The Walk

1 From the pub return to the road and turn right. In a few yards turn right again on a public footpath which is also the driveway to The Old Cartlodge Tea Rooms. Just before you reach the tea rooms your path turns right. Shortly, turn left at the back of the pub and keep to the left of some buildings to reach a stile which you cross. Bear right across a field towards a gate and after going through this, bear diagonally left across the next field, making for a stile in the fence ahead. As you go down a slope you will see the stile about 100 yards to the left of a farm gate and roughly in the middle of the fence. After crossing the stile, bear left downhill through woods. Where your path turns sharply right towards a road, turn left, still going through woods but now with fields on the right. Go over a stile and continue under trees, then, having crossed a second stile, turn sharply right to cross a third by a footpath sign. Turn left, now with a hedge on your left, and cross the next stile. Turn right onto a wide bridleway, soon going through a gate. In about 100 yards, turn left over a stile by a signpost

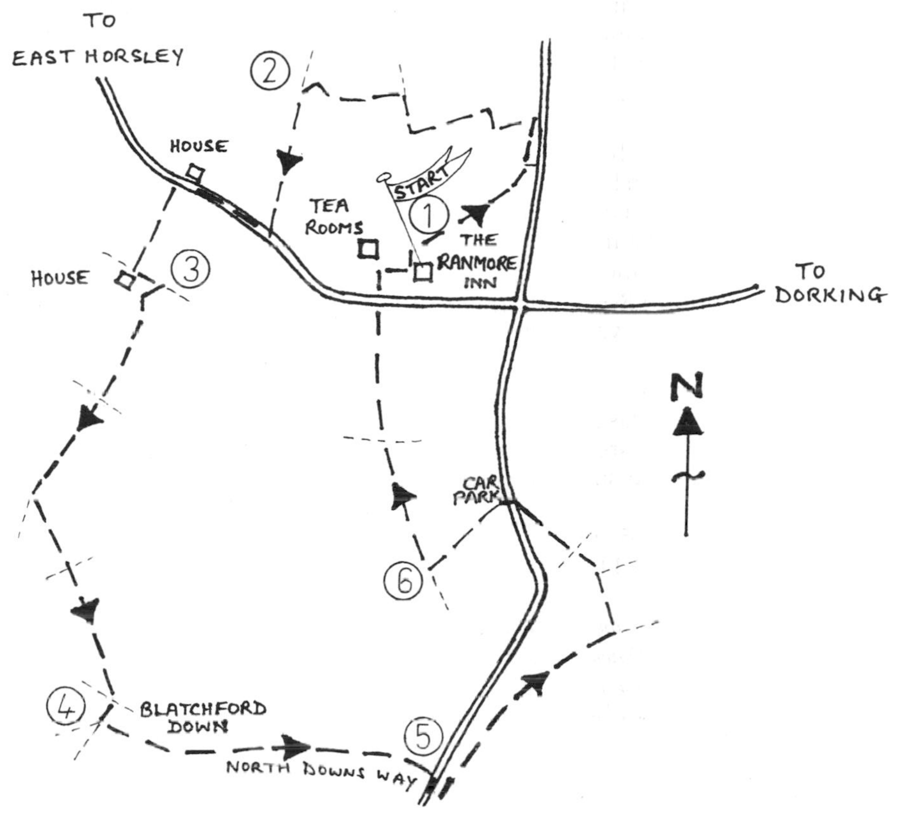

and head across a field with a wire fence on your left, crossing another stile at a fork. You bear right through a wood, passing along the side of a beautiful timbered house, The Old Malt House, to reach a T-junction.

2 Turn left on a bridleway and eventually reach the road once again. Turn right for about 300 yards and, after passing a house on your right, turn left on a public bridleway. You reach a T-junction by a house and turn left for about 100 yards, going through a gate.

3 Turn right through posts on a recently diverted bridleway and shortly reach a T-junction. Turn left and in about 200 yards go over a crossing track. In another 300 yards or so, and about 20 paces beyond a fire warning notice, turn left by a large yew tree onto a path running under trees. You go through some posts and in about 200 yards cross a wide crossing track to the path opposite. You may find some handy logs here if you are looking for a seat. Later a track comes in from the right and you continue ahead, shortly going over a crossing track and eventually arriving at a junction of paths.

4 Turn left over a stile, passing a sign indicating that you are on Blatchford Down and on the North Downs Way. If you are ready for a rest there is a handy seat over on your left. Pass a stile by a gate on your right and continue on, enjoying good views over to other Surrey hills, including Holmbury Hill, on your right. Pass another stile and gate on your right and, later, an old pillbox, also on the right. There is yet another stile/gate to pass and you ignore a left fork and continue following the acorn signs. Shortly after passing your fourth stile/gate combination, go through a bridle gate next to a farm gate. Ignore a right fork and continue to follow the acorns, with another pillbox down on your right. Stay with the meandering path, still on the North Downs Way, and eventually it goes sharply right and down to a road.

5 Turn right along the road for a few paces and then turn left up a slope, still on the North Downs Way. Following the contour of the slope, 656 ft above sea level, continue on the Way, shortly passing a brick pillbox on your left and a North Downs Way acorn on your right. You pass another brick pillbox on your right and about 200 yards beyond this reach a stile which you do not cross. Instead, turn left up a steep slope, later ignoring a right turn. You pass a large open area on your left and reach the top of the slope. Another track comes in from your right and you reach a wide crossing track by some fallen trees. Cross over to the narrow path opposite and bear left under the trees. This meandering path shortly brings you back out to the road. Cross to a small car park opposite (White Down) where you continue ahead on a wide bridleway for about 300 yards to reach a crossing track.

6 Turn right along this straight track and in about ¼ mile go over a crossing track. A few yards further on, reach a junction of tracks by a four-way fingerpost. Continue ahead on another dead straight bridleway. Go over a stile by a gate and reach the road. Turn right for a few yards and you are back at the driveway leading to the pub.

24 Shamley Green
The Red Lion

The Red Lion (freehouse) looks small but thinks big. The building was formerly the village store but has been a pub since Victorian times and is now licensed as a hotel and restaurant.

The pleasant restaurant has high standards of cuisine. Everything offered is home cooked – nothing at all is brought in. There are toasted sandwiches, or you might be tempted to try Green Thai Curry or grilled stuffed mushrooms topped with Brie. There are some good desserts, too. Being a hotel, food is available all day long. You could even have your breakfast here before (or after?) you start your walk. You will find real ales at the attractive bar, such as Flowers and Abbot, and they are changed as frequently as the menu – which is often. The cider is Red Rock. Children are welcome but dogs are not allowed inside. There is a large beer garden at the back which can be used on fine days throughout the entire year.

The opening hours are Monday to Saturday 10 am – midnight, Sunday 12 noon – 4 pm and 7 pm – 11.30 pm. Food is served every day 7 am – 10 pm.

Telephone: 0483 892202.

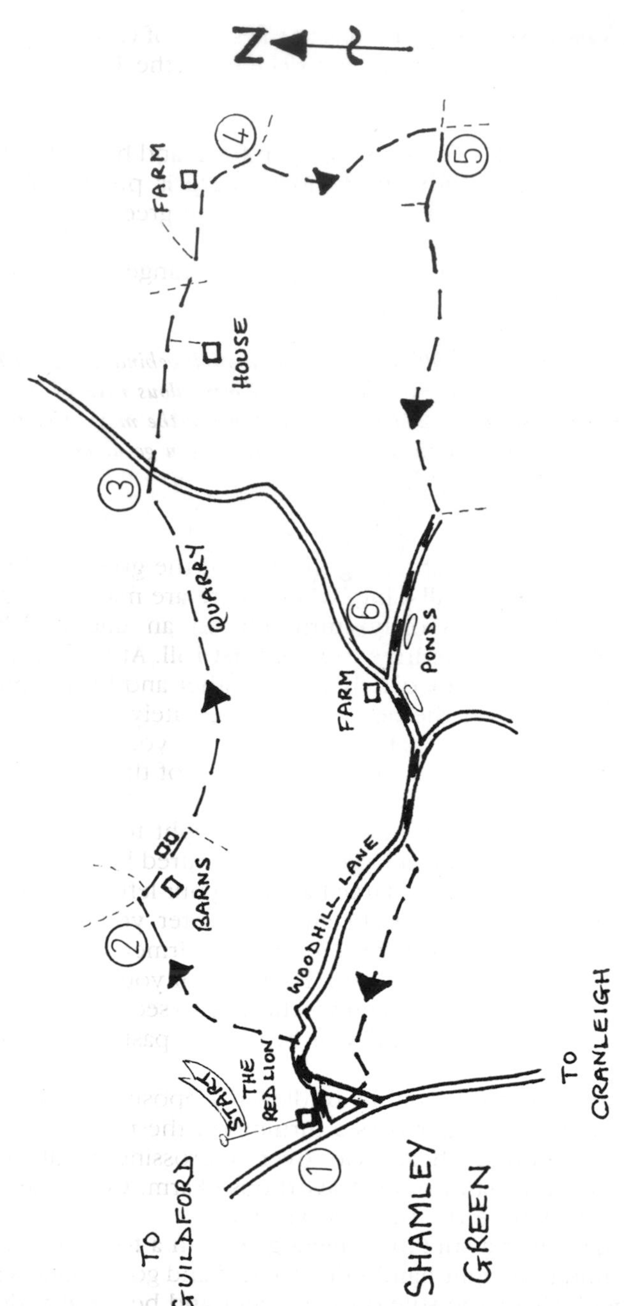
N
FARM
4
5
HOUSE
3
QUARRY
6
PONDS
FARM
BARNS
2
WOODHILL LANE
START
THE RED LION
1
TO GUILDFORD
SHAMLEY GREEN
TO CRANLEIGH

How to get there: Shamley Green is to the south of Guildford. The pub is on the village green, which is bisected by the B2128 running to Cranleigh.

Parking: The pub has limited parking in front and behind, which you are welcome to use with permission. There is plenty of additonal parking on the little roads that criss-cross the green.

Length of the walk: 4 miles. OS maps: Landranger 186 and 187 or Pathfinder 1226 (GR 031438).

You soon leave the small village by climbing the hill behind it, from which there are pleasant views north and south. Surrey has a marvellous network of bridleways, many used by our forefathers, and you explore some of the most attractive, passing the occasional horse rider, or even fellow walker, as you go along.

The Walk

1 From the pub turn left along the side of the green and at the far end turn left up Woodhill Lane, where there are many attractive and interesting buildings. Shortly, turn left on an enclosed footpath running parallel with the drive to Sandhurst Hill. At the top of a slope go over a stile, then immediately over another and bear slightly right across a field and over the next stile. Immediately cross another and then follow an enclosed path with a field on your right. Your path becomes even more enclosed and, at the top of the slope, you reach a T-junction.

2 Look back at the views and then turn right to continue along a bridleway, shortly passing a large cream-coloured barn on your right, soon followed by two more large barns on your left. You should have good views over to your right and left. Later you should find an alternative parallel track on the left which is firmer and will save you the effort of walking in deep sand. However, if you keep on the main track and climb a small bank you will be able to see a huge sand quarry below. The tracks merge and you bear right past a gate to reach a road.

3 Cross the road to the public bridleway opposite which is also the drive to Kilnhanger. Later pass a turning on the right leading to the house and continue ahead. Go over a crossing bridleway, later ignoring a left fork, and reach Mayorhouse Farm. Continue for a 100 yards or so to where the track curves left.

4 Turn right over a stile by a metal gate with a footpath fingerpost. Continue along the right-hand side of a field and go through a gate into another field. Cross the stile on your right and bear right, down to a sandy bridleway. Turn left along the bridleway which skirts the edge of a wood. Ignore a right turn and, in about another 300 yards, reach a wide crossing track.

5 Turn right along the track, which shortly goes down a slope, becomes deeply rutted, and is potentially muddy. Remain on this bridleway for about ½ mile where you will reach a cottage and a road. Continue ahead on the road and later pass an attractive, reed-fringed pond on your left to reach another road at a T-junction by Woodhill Farm.

6 Turn left along the road, with great care, and shortly you will pass another attractive pond on your left. Cross over the turning to Cranleigh on the left and, when the road curves to the right, turn left at a signpost onto a public footpath which is also the driveway to Reel Hall. Shortly, pass the very fine house on your right. Reach a fork by Little Cucknells and bear right. Continue on the tarred driveway which forms part of the Greensand Way for about ¼ mile, passing stables, and then look out for a metal gate on your left where you join a narrow, enclosed path. Shortly pass a stile on your left, thus leaving the Greensand Way and then go over the next stile. You continue on an extremely narrow path running between holly bushes and a high, wooden fence. Later the path turns left and then right and you emerge back onto the village green where you bear right over towards the pub.

25 Shere
The White Horse

The White Horse (Chef and Brewer) is a most attractive pub, popular with locals and visitors alike. The building dates from 1475 and has been an alehouse, coaching inn and public house for the past 300 years. Although owned by one of the country's largest brewing and leisure chains, it retains the charm of a typical British country inn for which we are world famous. During excavations in the last century a cellar wall was removed and kegs of illicit brandy discovered. We are not aware whether the excise duty was subsequently paid but can, unfortunately, report that none of the vintage liquor is still available at the bar! There are several nooks and crannies where you may find a seat, but on sunny Sunday lunchtimes the pub almost bursts at the seams.

All the food is home-made and there are ten or more choices on the blackboard, with fish a speciality. Three or four dishes are available all day long. You will also find several types of ploughman's, chunky sandwiches and other pub snacks. The real ales are Ruddles – County and Best – and Yorkshire Bitter has found its way here, too. The cider comes up from Somerset, bearing the Strongbow label.

The opening hours are Monday to Saturday 11 am – 11 pm, Sunday 12 noon – 3 pm and 7 pm – 10.30 pm. The main menu is available on Monday to Saturday 12 noon – 2 pm and 7 pm – 9.30 pm, and on Sunday 12 noon – 2 pm and 7 pm – 9 pm, with a reduced menu at other times.

Telephone: 0483 202518.

How to get there: Leave the A25, between Guildford and Dorking, at either of the two signs for Shere. Turn into the village main street (Middle Street) and find the pub on the right.

Parking: The pub has no parking of its own and Shere is congested with parked vehicles at the best of times. Try the road opposite leading up to the church or go to the recreation ground car park at the other end of the village.

Length of the walk: 4 miles. OS maps: Landranger 187 or Pathfinder 1226 (GR 073478).

In an area steeped in history, this is an extremely pleasant walk, starting and finishing in one of the quaintest villages of Surrey's heartland. Once you climb out of the busy little village you will discover tranquillity at its best, being alone with your thoughts whilst the world hurries by below.

The Walk

1 From the pub take the road opposite and shortly go through the Lutyens-designed lychgate leading to St James's church. Fork left and pass the church on your right. Towards the far end of the churchyard, at a T-junction, turn left and use a footbridge taking you over the Tillingbourne. Continue over a green, with a small public open-air swimming pool over on your left, and come out to a road. Cross the road, turn left and pass a restaurant on your right, the former Oak Cottage. You reach the Village Hall and turn right between this and the Village Club to come to a recreation ground. Turn left through a car park and go through the gates at the end.

2 Turn right onto a wide, sunken track and shortly ignore a left fork. Go under the A25 and, a few yards further on, turn sharp left up to another track where you turn right. The track you left is now below you on the right. Commence climbing steadily uphill and, where the path bears left, catch your breath and pause for a bird's eye view back over Shere below. Continue to climb, often glancing back to your left for more fine views. The climb becomes a little more steep and the path quite stony. Later the path is enclosed. There is a wire fence and a field on your left. Take heart, you are close to the summit now. The

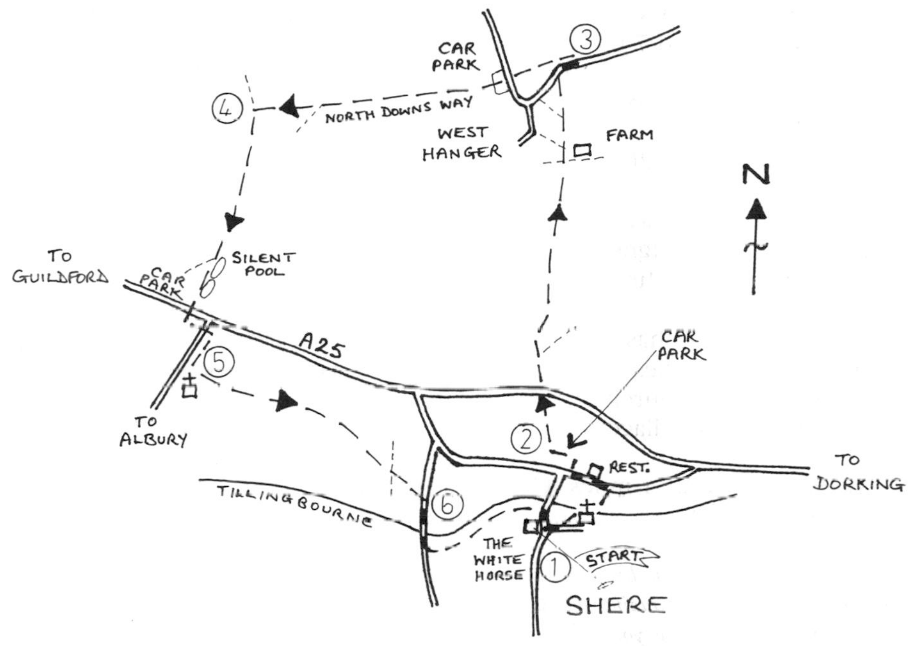

path levels out at last and two cottages come into view. Go over a crossing track by the entrance to Hollister Farm. Ignore a sloping fork to the left and continue ahead on what you will see from the acorn marker is part of the North Downs Way. Ignore the next left fork, remaining on the North Downs Way and eventually coming out to a road. Cross the road and turn right, continuing along it for a few yards with care.

3 Turn left at the North Downs Way fingerpost and pass a rather sorry-looking pond on your right. Continue on this track for 250 yards and reach another road which you cross to West Hanger car park. After crossing the car park pick up the track, a former drove road. After ¼ mile or so ignore a left fork and continue ahead passing some Surrey County Council signs. In about another 300 yards pass a small concrete bridleway sign and come to a crossing track.

4 Turn left on the public footpath, marked with a 'bovine' sign, and a little green post with a figure '5', thus leaving the North Downs Way. Commence your descent from the North Downs, often enjoying some good views on the way, but watch your feet, too, as this path can be slippery. Ignore several little turnings to the left until you reach another small post, this one numbered '6'. Here turn left and shortly reach a T-junction where you turn right, down some steps leading you to the Silent Pool. Turn right, with the pool on your left. Pass a wooden boathouse and continue along the side of the sister Sherbourne Pond. Go through a gate and turn left through a car park to the A25. Cross the road with great care and turn left and then cross the road to Godalming and Albury. Turn right along an enclosed path running parallel with the road and reach a gate from which you will obtain a good view of the spectacular Catholic Apostolic Church, now long closed although still well maintained.

5 Turn left on the upward-sloping public footpath and shortly go over a stile leading you into the grounds of Albury Park. Go over a large, grassy field and over another stile then ahead and under trees. You leave the woods via a gate and continue straight across the next field passing a very tall wall over on your right. Go over a crossing track, back into woods and down to a lane.

6 Turn right, shortly passing a most attractive black and white, timbered cottage. Pass a pond on your left and cross a bridge by a ford. Turn left through a gate and continue with the Tillingbourne down on your left. Go through another gate and turn left, soon passing a turning on the left. Pass another turning on the left by a ford and footbridge and continue ahead on the road. Look for an unusual, overhanging building on the right, the Old Prison, and shortly you will be back in Shere village centre with The White Horse on your right.

26 Sutton Abinger
The Volunteer

The Volunteer (freehouse), which has always been popular with walkers, takes its name from the time when it was used as the main recruiting station between Dorking and Guildford during the Boer and First World Wars. The building dates from 1630 and became an alehouse over 150 years ago when it supplied beer and home-made bread and cheese to the farming community. Many of the farming implements of that era are displayed in the bar and highly polished barrels serve as stylish seats. To illustrate the military connection memorabilia is also displayed on the walls.

You can eat in the attractively beamed, Tudor dining-room which has been formed from a previous kitchen and pot room. The varied menu of good home-cooked pub grub is all on the blackboard and changes daily. There are puddings, too, most of which are home-made. For serious beer-drinkers, Sussex, Tetley, Benskins and Burton are available. Cider drinkers should try the Copperhead; but be warned – not too much! Well-behaved dogs and children are allowed in the bar and outside there is a pretty, terraced garden with lovely views and a play area. For those not wanting to tear themselves away from the area accommodation is available – one double and two twin bedrooms which, naturally, come with a hearty, full English breakfast.

The opening hours are Monday to Friday 11 am–3 pm and 6 pm–11 pm, Saturday 11 am–11 pm, and Sunday 12 noon–3 pm and 7 pm–10.30 pm. Food is served on Monday to Saturday 12 noon–2 pm and 6.30 pm–9.30 pm, and on Sunday 12 noon–2 pm and 7 pm–9.30 pm.

Telephone: 0306 730798.

How to get there: Leave the A25, between Guildford and Dorking, at Abinger Hammer by going south on Felday Road (B2126), signposted to Holmbury St Mary. You will reach Sutton Abinger in about 1½ miles where you turn left to the pub, which will be in view.

Parking: The pub has an adequate car park which you are welcome to use whilst you take your walk, but please park at the far end and let someone know you are there.

Length of the walk: 4 miles. OS maps: Landranger 187 or Pathfinder 1226 (GR 105459).

This is a fairly gentle walk in pleasant countryside with woodland and farmland. Although there are no climbs (just one fairly steep decline), you will have some fine views across to the North Downs. Starting out from one hamlet, you will also visit another with a church that has an unusual story of modern times to tell.

The Walk

1 From the pub turn left to the road and then right to the road junction. Turn right down the road for about 100 yards and then turn left up a sloping footpath running between wire fences. You come out to a lane by Stile Cottage and turn left for a few yards and then right on a path marked 'SCC No Horses'. Continue on the path with a large field over on your left and reach a lane by a fingerpost. Turn left, continuing on the lane for about 300 yards where you reach a road on the right opposite a notice board for Sutton Place.

2 Turn right on an enclosed public footpath, shortly with a conifer hedge on your right. Continue ahead on a tarred driveway and then a grassy path leading down to a stile. Go down some steps, continue straight ahead towards a line of trees, then go up a slope and cross a stile. Head across a field, making for another stile on the far side. Cross the stile and continue on a track, with a market garden on the left, leading you out to a lane.

3 Turn left, soon ignoring a turning on the right, and continue on this wide track as it bears left. Follow the bridleway which is also the drive to Silton. When this bears left, you go straight ahead onto

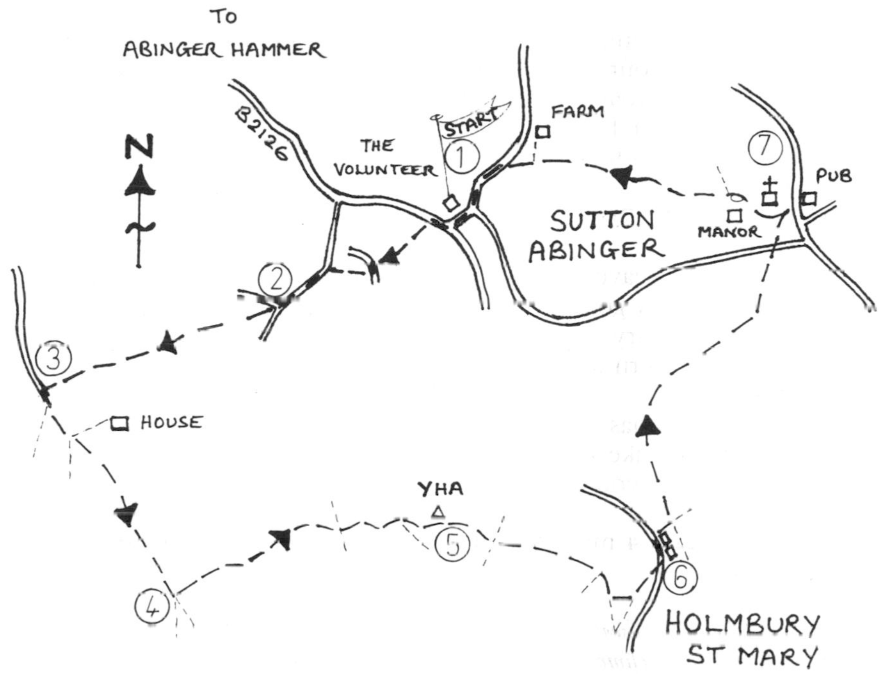

another track which, after rain, is liable to be quite muddy. Continue up the slope and remain on this track for almost another ½ mile, passing some vast badger earthworks on the way. When you reach the end of a large field on your left and a smaller one on the right, you come to a fork where you bear left to a crossing track.

4 Turn left, with the large field remaining on your left, and when you reach a gate marked 'Private – No Right of Way', bear right. You soon pass a turning on the left and reach a main track on which you turn left. Ignore the more sunken track down on your left and turnings to the left and right as your track descends to a wider one, which you cross. Pass a pond on your right and bear left up the slope. Where you reach a junction of tracks, do not bear right with the main track but leave it, maintaining your original direction with a fence on your left, and reach a small car park. The Holmbury St Mary Youth Hostel is on the other side of the car park.

5 Continue ahead, go over a crossing track by a large Scots pine and down a slope to a wide crossing track. Your path climbs and then levels out. Pass a main turning on the right and 50 yards beyond this, where the path starts to descend, look for an easily missed narrow path on the left. Turn left downhill, ignoring a branching path to the left. Your path now goes steeply downhill to a crossing track with houses ahead. Here you turn turn left and shortly come out to a road at a 30 mph sign close to the village of Holmbury St Mary.

6 Cross the road with care and turn left. After passing a row of houses on your right, turn right across a small parking area. Shortly, pass a disused swimming pool, formed by the damming of a water course, and reach a crossing track with a stile ahead. Do not cross the stile but turn left over another stile, with a yellow paint mark, by a gate. Remain on this wide track as it bears to the right and ignore a wide right turn. At a fork go left, i.e. not following the cable line above. Ignore a small path branching right and continue up a slope, joining a path coming in from the right. You reach a stile which you cross. Head straight over a field, then cross a road over to the green by Abinger church. There is another pub here, The Abinger Hatch, but you are not more than 20 minutes away from where your car is parked.

7 Turn left through a gate, passing the church on your immediate right and leave the churchyard via another gate leading you onto an enclosed path. Pass Abinger Manor and its pond on your left, soon with sweeping views over to your right. Cross a stile and, ignoring a right fork, continue straight ahead across a field. Go through a gateway, over a cattle grid, and shortly along an enclosed track. Where the track turns right into a farmyard, go straight ahead over a stile by a gate. Continue on the path, with a holly hedge over on your right, and once over the next stile go down some steps to a lane. Turn left, downhill, and very shortly you will be back at the pub.

27 Tilford
The Duke of Cambridge

The Duke of Cambridge (freehouse) is relatively new for a pub and only traces its history back to the turn of the century. The L-shaped room, with its attractive corner bar, has a cosy, roaring fire at each end in winter. This is a small, friendly house with no pretensions to being a gourmet restaurant.

The food served is good, basic pub grub. Chicken dishes are the speciality, but if you are really hungry go for the 'All-Day Breakfast'. Something we have never found elsewhere – and certainly rather unusual for a pub – is its offer of free coffee served with any meal. The real ale regulars are Courage Best and Marston's Pedigree and there are usually two or three others on offer. Cider drinkers can choose between Dry Blackthorn and Scrumpy Jack. Children are welcome and dogs are also, if kept on leads. Outside there is a pleasant garden, with a play area for children, and barbecues are held on fine summer evenings.

The opening hours are Monday to Friday 11 am–3 pm and 5.30 pm–11 pm, Saturday 11 am–11 pm, and Sunday 12 noon–3 pm and 7 pm–10.30 pm. Food is served on Monday to Saturday 12 noon–2.30 pm and 6 pm–10 pm ,and on Sunday 12 noon–2.20 pm and 7 pm–9.30 pm.

Telephone: 0252 792236.

How to get there: Tilford lies south-east of Farnham, off the B3001. From the green, take the road going south for about ¾ mile and find the pub on the left by the entrance to Hankley Common Golf Club. If travelling north, take Tilford Road from Rushmoor and find the pub on the right after about ¾ mile.

Parking: There is an adequate car park which you are welcome to use whilst on the walk.

Length of the walk: 3½ miles. OS maps: Landranger 186 or Pathfinder 1225 (GR 876425).

This is Surrey heathland at its best. You will enjoy many views over the wilder areas of this part of the county, but will nevertheless be keeping to well-defined paths. Even after heavy rain you should not find muddy patches, but be prepared for a few stretches of soft sand and choose suitable footwear. This area is used by the military for training purposes, so do not be surprised if you are suddenly confronted by a platoon of Gurkhas, or the like. You are warned not to touch suspicious-looking objects, but the only hazard you might possibly encounter is an ill-aimed, low-flying golf ball – so look out!

The Walk

1 From the pub turn right on a track leading to Hankley Common Golf Club. Just before reaching the clubhouse, turn left across a car park. Pick up a track leading from some posts and continue along the side of a fairway. The track later touches on woodland and you bear left to reach Stockbridge Pond. Continue forward a few yards to reach a small parking area and a T-junction.

2 Turn right and pass a sign indicating that you are entering a military training area. The track bears to the right and, at a junction of three tracks, take the one on the right which soon becomes sunken. When you reach a more open area, continue ahead on the right fork and soon you will come to another fork where you bear right by a post. Continue over a crossing track on the side of Yagden Hill and at another junction of paths go straight ahead. You will soon reach the outer limits of the golf course on your right and, at a further junction of paths, you maintain direction uphill.

3 At the 11th tee, turn left on a wide crossing track and, soon after reaching a fenced enclosure on your left, turn right. Continue uphill

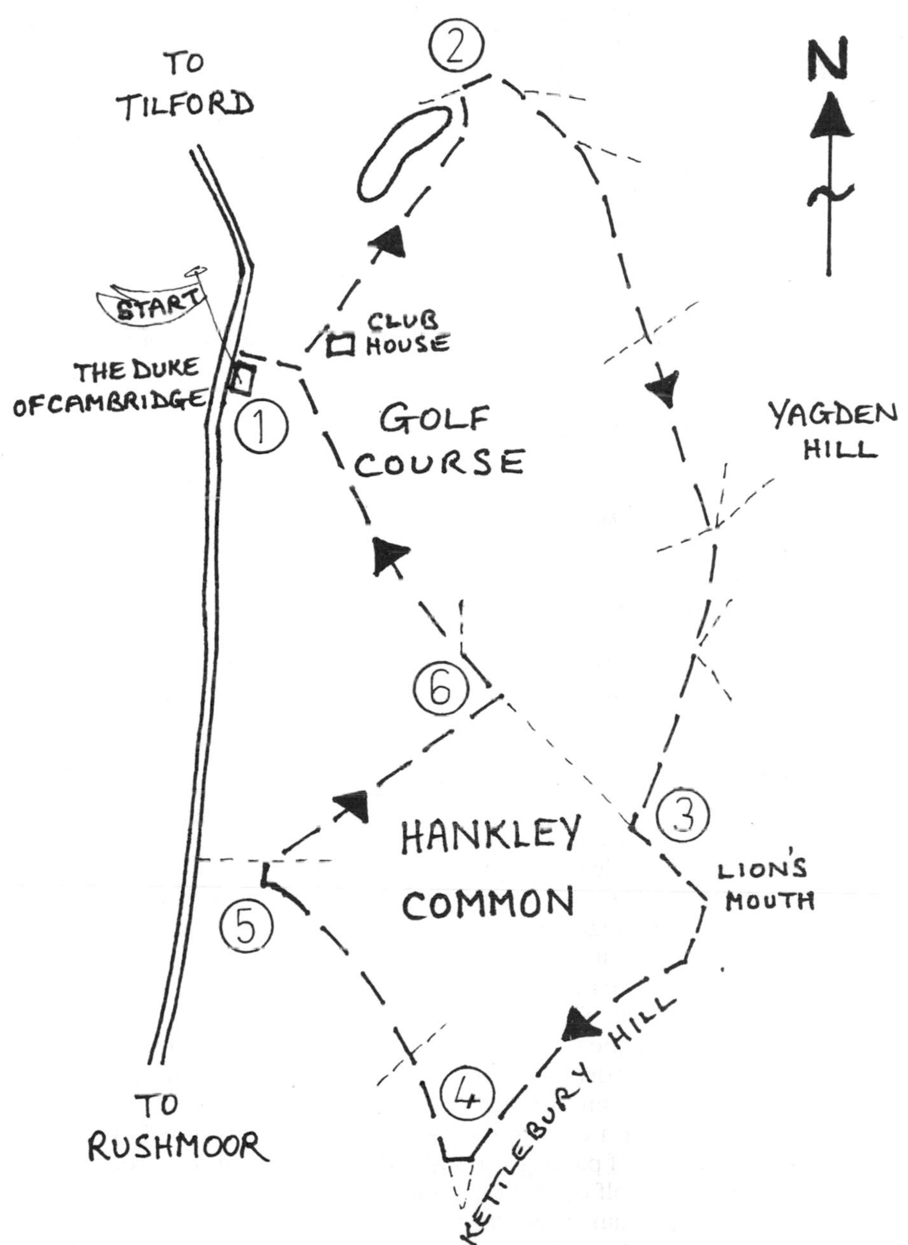
TO
TILFORD
N
START
THE DUKE
OF CAMBRIDGE
CLUB
HOUSE
GOLF
COURSE
YAGDEN
HILL
HANKLEY
COMMON
LION'S
MOUTH
KETTLEBURY HILL
TO
RUSHMOOR

on an even wider sandy track leading you up Kettlebury Hill. The area is known as the Lion's Mouth. At the top of the slope, turn right on a fine ridge path. For about ½ mile you will enjoy excellent views to the left towards Thursley Common and occasionally to the right over Hankley Common. Where the track curves to the left you should find a turning on the right.

4 Turn right through the trees and in about 100 yards meet a wide crosssing track. Turn right, shortly passing a public bridleway sign, and continue down a slope. At the bottom go over a wide crossing track, then up a slope and down again. Continue on to a junction of paths on the edge of some more golfing greens.

5 Turn right alongside a post-and-rail barrier and, in about 100 yards, turn right onto a bridleway at an ancient fingerpost. There is a fairway on your right as you continue along this track for almost another ½ mile, and about 100 yards before a wooden hut, reach a waymarked crossing track.

6 Turn left, shortly ignoring a right fork. Remembering your green cross code, continue over a fairway! You reach a T-junction, with a caravan park beyond, and turn right, shortly passing the clubhouse once more. Bear left, back to the pub.

28 Westcott
The Cricketers

The Cricketers (freehouse), rather strangely called The Wizard for a short time, has also served as a bakehouse and a laundry. It then became a 'bottle and jug', a forerunner of today's off-licence. This is an unpretentious pub on three levels, one of them being a cosy area for diners.

You will find typical, good pub grub, including ploughman's, toasted sandwiches, an excellent home-cooked steak and kidney pie, as well as steaks and fish and chips. You will not go hungry – portions here are generous – and your wallet will not get too much of a shock either. The real ales are Badger Best, Tanglefoot, Brakspear, Boddingtons and London Pride. Draught cider addicts will be offered Strongbow straight from the barrel. Children and well-behaved dogs are welcome. There is no garden but if you want to sit in the sunshine there are a couple of tables in front of the house.

The opening hours are Monday to Saturday 11 am–3 pm and 5.30 pm–11 pm, Sunday 12 noon–3 pm and 7 pm–10.30 pm. Food is served on Monday to Saturday 12 noon–2 pm and 7 pm–9 pm (not Monday or Wednesday evenings), and on Sunday 12 noon–2 pm and 7.30 pm–9 pm.

Telephone: 0306 883520.

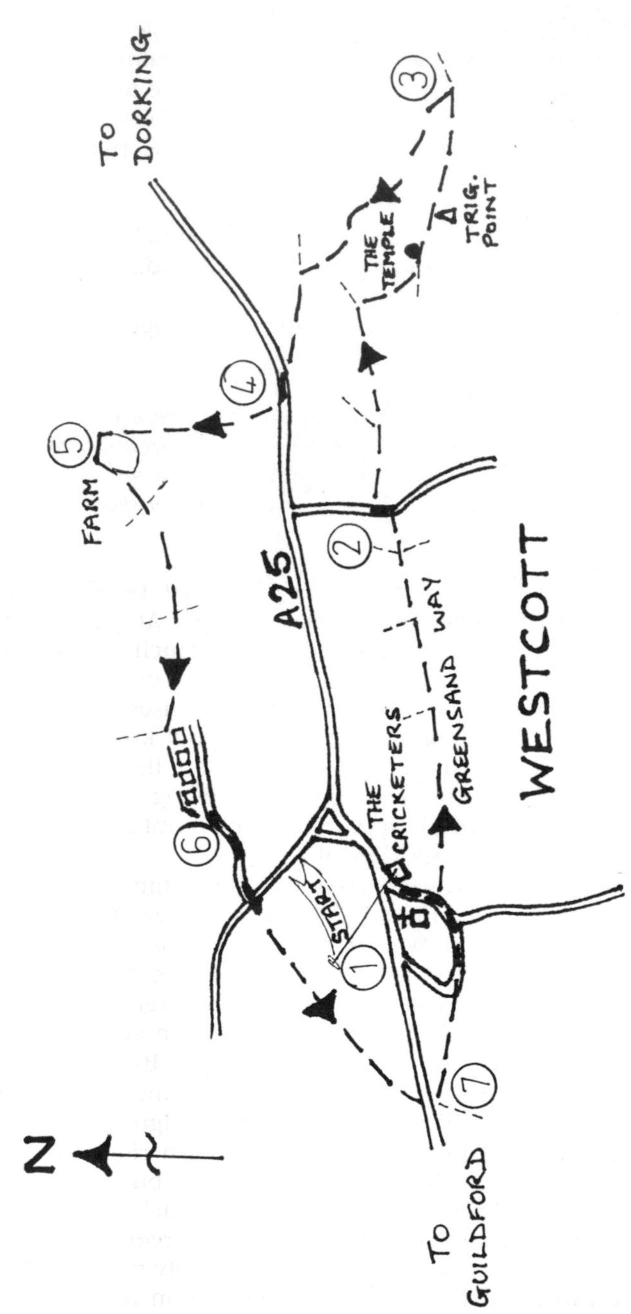
TO DORKING
TO GUILDFORD
A25
WESTCOTT
GREENSAND WAY
THE CRICKETERS
THE TEMPLE
TRIG. POINT
FARM
START
N
1
2
3
4
5
6
7

How to get there: Westcott is on the A25 a couple of miles to the west of Dorking, and the pub is easily spotted. If coming from Dorking you should look carefully for the pub's sign on the left at the far end of the village. If you are entering the village from the Guildford direction, look out for the church on the right and the pub is immediately beyond this.

Parking: The pub has no parking area of its own but space will usually be found on the right-hand side of the lane leading up to the church.

Length of the walk: 4 miles. OS maps: Landranger 187 or Pathfinder 1226 (GR 140485).

The walk circles the attractive village of Westcott, which you may like to explore afterwards. The east-west part of the route follows the Greensand Way and includes a short climb up to The Temple, an elegant circular seat from where you can have an excellent view over Dorking, with its graceful church spire.

The Walk

1 From the pub continue up the lane past Holy Trinity church, designed by Sir George Gilbert Scott in 1852. At the top of the slope turn sharply left on a public footpath which forms part of the Greensand Way. You reach some houses and continue ahead, past a fence on your left. You pass some more houses and remain on the enclosed path, shortly going through a metal kissing-gate. Continue on, passing two footpath turnings on your left, then go over a crossing track with gates on either side, still following the Greensand Way. Continue until you reach an attractive half-timbered house, then go over a footbridge to a residential road.

2 Turn left for 50 yards or so where you will find some steps on your right and a sign indicating a link route between the Greensand Way and the North Downs Way. Go up the steps and continue on an enclosed path between paddocks. You reach a cottage and go forward on a driveway leading you onto a tarred lane. Ignore a turning on the left. The lane curves to the left and at an open area on the right you turn right, still following the Greensand Way. By two large oak trees on your right, temporarily leave the Greensand Way by ignoring a steep left fork and taking a path to the right. Ignore a turning on the right and reach a T-junction where you turn right. At a very large chestnut tree turn left through rhododendron bushes and pass an old brick and flint wall on your right. Shortly a track comes in from your right and you soon bear right, rejoining the Greensand Way at a post. Shortly you reach a covered seat, appropriately named 'The Temple'. Rest here awhile to take in the good views in many directions and particularly what looks like a toy town Dorking with its impressive church spire. Continue along your path, shortly passing an old triangulation point on your right. Later the path divides and you bear left, almost immediately finding a turning on the left.

3 Turn sharp left on a downward sloping path and go over a small crossing track, bearing left and still going downhill. At a junction of several paths continue straight ahead and at the ensuing fork keep right. Go over another small crossing track, and then a wide crossing track, eventually reaching a T-junction where you turn right. Go through some wooden posts to a crossing track (with a large car park beyond) and turn left. Pass a house and two stone posts, going over the lane you were on earlier. Continue ahead on the footpath under trees and eventually reach the main road (A25). Go left along the road for a few yards and then, with great care, cross over to a turning on the right, leading to an insurance company's offices.

4 Turn right on the bridleway. There is a stream running down on your left and you reach an attractive lake. As you approach an ornate gateway, turn left and cross over a bridge to a farmyard and immediate left turn.

5 Turn left through the farmyard on a very rough track, passing some large barns on your right. Go through a kissing-gate leading you into a field and walk straight across it and over a stile. There are good views of the North Downs over on your right. Go straight across the next field to another stile by a gate. Continue on an enclosed path, cross over another stile and pass along the side of a field with houses on your left. Ignore a small footpath and footbridge on your left and go over a crossing track, with a bridge on the left and a stile over on the right. At the end of this field go over a barrier and footbridge, turning left between houses and coming out to a residential road.

6 Turn right along the road and reach another road, which you cross to a narrow, enclosed path running between hedges. Later you will be passing an attractive lake on your right and will have glimpses of it through the hedge. Eventually you reach the A25 again, crossing over it to the entrance of Rookery Drive.

7 Turn left on a footpath, back again on the Greensand Way. Shortly, pass some very sandy banks on your left and continue on an upward slope which becomes a driveway and leads you out to a lane. Cross the lane, soon reaching a green (this is Westcott Heath) with seats on the left and attractive houses over to your right. Your path continues under trees and brings you out to the lane where you commenced your walk. Turn left past the church, back to the pub.

29 Westhumble
The Stepping Stones

The Stepping Stones (Friary Meux) is named after the alternative, fun way of crossing the nearby river Mole. It is very conveniently situated for those wanting a walk embracing Surrey's most famous viewpoint on Box Hill and has always been popular with walkers. Plastic bags are provided in the doorway for muddy boots! There is a separate dining-room with an area for non-smokers and a large, comfortable bar area.

You will find an extensive menu of reasonably priced meals for the evening and a large menu of bar meals, including dishes of the day, sandwiches and baked potatoes with toppings. An innovative 'Build Your Own Pizza' option is available all day. Real ales include Burton Ale, Friary Best and a weekly changed guest ale. Olde English cider is also on tap. Children are welcome but dogs must remain in the pleasant garden area.

The opening hours are Monday to Saturday 11 am – 2.30 pm and 5.30 pm–11 pm, Sunday 12 noon–3 pm and 7 pm–10.30 pm. Food is served all the time (last orders 30 minutes before closing).

Telephone: 0306 889932.

How to get there: From the A24 Leatherhead–Dorking road turn into Westhumble Street, signposted to Boxhill and Westhumble station. The pub is on the immediate left and the railway station is only a couple of minutes' walk away.

Parking: Space is limited but, if you ask permission, you are welcome to park your car and return later for your meal. Just a few minutes away there is a large public car park on the other side of the A24 near the Burford Bridge Hotel (not the hotel car park).

Length of the walk: 5 miles. OS maps: Landranger 187 or Pathfinder 1206 (GR 170517).

A favourite picnic spot for centuries, Box Hill offers serene beauty, unchanged by the passage of time. The walk explores a lesser-known route to what is regarded as one of the most spectacular viewpoints on the North Downs. There is a long, gradual ascent and a shorter, slightly steeper descent with the aid of steps, but the view at the top makes both worthwhile.

The Walk

1 From the pub car park turn left along the road. Where the pavement ends continue carefully and, a little later, cross a bridge by Boxhill and Westhumble railway station. Immediately over the railway bridge you will see an archway ahead with a chapel on the right, but you continue the walk before reaching it by turning right on a footpath, at first enclosed. Go through a gate and continue along the right-hand edge of a field with the railway over on your right. Later Norbury Park House, once the home of Marie Stopes, comes into view on the hill over on your left. The river Mole is then crossed by an iron bridge and you continue for another 100 yards.

2 Turn right under the railway arch and go ahead to a road. Cross over the dual carriageway (A24), with great care, to an enclosed footpath. Go through a metal gate, cross the drive to Fredley Manor and go over the stile opposite. Cross a field, keeping a fence on your right, go through a kissing-gate into another field and continue with the trees on your right. Climb the steps ahead and follow the path to a road. Turn right, along the pavement, and in 50 yards continue on a footpath running parallel to the road. Juniper Hall, now a field studies centre, can shortly be seen across the road on your left. Follow the footpath to its end where you go down some steps to rejoin the pavement at a fingerpost.

3 Cross the road and go up the drive opposite. Continue ahead, passing Little Pinehurst and ignore any right forks. Later your grassy path goes quite steeply downhill to meet a crossing track at the

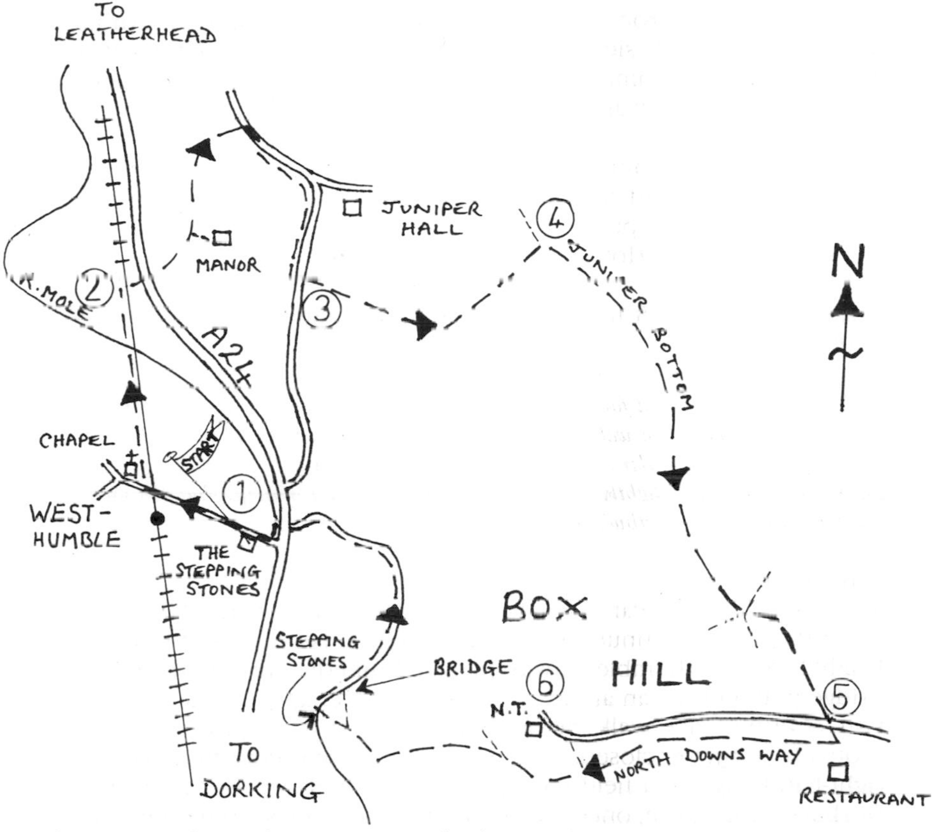

bottom with a stile opposite, which you do not cross.

4 Turn right and walk up the open valley path of Juniper Bottom for nearly a mile, going straight ahead up the hill and through trees, ignoring crossing tracks. On reaching a fence, continue ahead, keeping it on your left, and come out to a road.

5 Cross over the road to enter the car park for La Collina restaurant and soon turn right onto a stony track leading into a wooded area. After 25 yards turn right off the track onto a footpath with an acorn marker for the North Downs Way. Follow the footpath, keeping roughly parallel to the road, and eventually come down to a T-junction. Turn right and soon reach the Box Hill viewpoint. If you wish to use the National Trust shop, toilets and refreshment facility, fork right past the viewpoint and continue ahead along the road for 100 yards. Then retrace your steps.

6 From the viewpoint continue along the path towards the next acorn sign and, soon after, reach a turning on the left. From here you commence your steep descent, made easier by several flights of steps. At the bottom you reach a turning on the right and here you have the choice of crossing the river Mole via stepping stones by continuing ahead, or via the bridge by going right. Either way, after crossing the river, turn right and continue along the riverside path. You eventually reach a gate leading out to the main road. Turn left and use the pedestrian subway to take you under the road, then turn left and immediately right, back to the pub.

30 Wonersh
The Grantley Arms

The Grantley Arms (Friary Meux) has been a pub since the beginning of the century. Part of the building dates from the 17th century and is Grade I listed. There are plenty of exposed beams which are attractively lit and reflected on highly polished tables.

There is a separate restaurant with a non-smoking area but the bar is a fine place to dine, whether you are having a bar snack, a choice from one of the daily specials of home-cooked food, or something extra special from the comprehensive à la carte menu. The range is extensive, from burgers and basket meals through to several choices of succulent steaks. Children's portions are available. Tables in the bar can be reserved for small groups. Real ale lovers are well served with Friary, Tetley, Wadworth 6X and a guest beer. Draught Strongbow is available for those who prefer it. There is seating outside for warmer days. Children are welcome everywhere, but dogs are not allowed in the pub.

The opening hours are Monday to Friday 11 am–2.30 pm and 6 pm–11 pm, Saturday 11 am–3 pm and 6 pm–11 pm, and Sunday 12 noon–3 pm and 7 pm–10.30 pm. Food is served on Monday to Saturday 12 noon–2 pm and 6 pm–10 pm, and on Sunday 12 noon–2.15 pm and 7 pm–9.30 pm.

Telephone: 0483 893351.

How to get there: Wonersh lies south-east of Guildford. The pub is in a prominent position, in the centre of the village, where the B2128 meets the B2129, and cannot be missed.

Parking: The pub has a reasonably sized car park which, at most times, you would be welcome to use whilst you take your walk. Check first, in case your visit clashes with a function.

Length of the walk: 2½ miles. OS maps: Landranger 186 or Pathfinder 1226 (GR 017452).

This short ramble through the village of Wonersh, with its attractive buildings, continues with a leisurely climb, on a very convenient zigzag path, to the top of Chinthurst Hill, where you will be rewarded with good views in almost all directions. Rest awhile on one of the well-placed fallen tree trunks and imagine the even more splendid view that would have been afforded to the past landowner when he used his lofty folly, now, sadly, bricked up.

The Walk

1 From the pub cross the road and turn right, shortly bearing left into Barnett Lane and continue up this residential road. The village common soon comes into view on your left. When you arrive at the top of the road, cross over another and take the path opposite by a telephone kiosk. Continue ahead on the enclosed path and eventually reach a kissing-gate. Turn left, then immediately right by a three-way fingerpost. There is now a field on your right and a good view of St Martha's Hill ahead. You reach a T-junction with the impressive tithe barn of Tangley Manor just ahead.

2 Turn left on the track which forms part of the Downs Link Path, which joins the North Downs Way with the South Downs Way near Steyning. The route is waymarked with the distinctive 'double bridge' logo. About 100 yards before you reach the main road ahead bear right, still following the Downs Link signs. Ignore a turning on the left and eventually come out to a road, which you cross.

3 Take the public bridleway, passing Falcon Cottage over on your left. You reach a turning to the right, which you ignore, thus leaving the Downs Link. Go straight ahead on the path to 'The Tower'. You arrive at some steps and continue ahead to a longer flight and, at the top of this, reach a post where you turn left onto a permissive path. Commence the zigzag route, which will eventually take you to a crossing track by a seat. Cross to some more steps and at the top bear right to the summit of Chinthurst Hill with its attractive tower.

4 After you have rested awhile and enjoyed the views, continue ahead and, very shortly, bear right downhill over a grassy area with

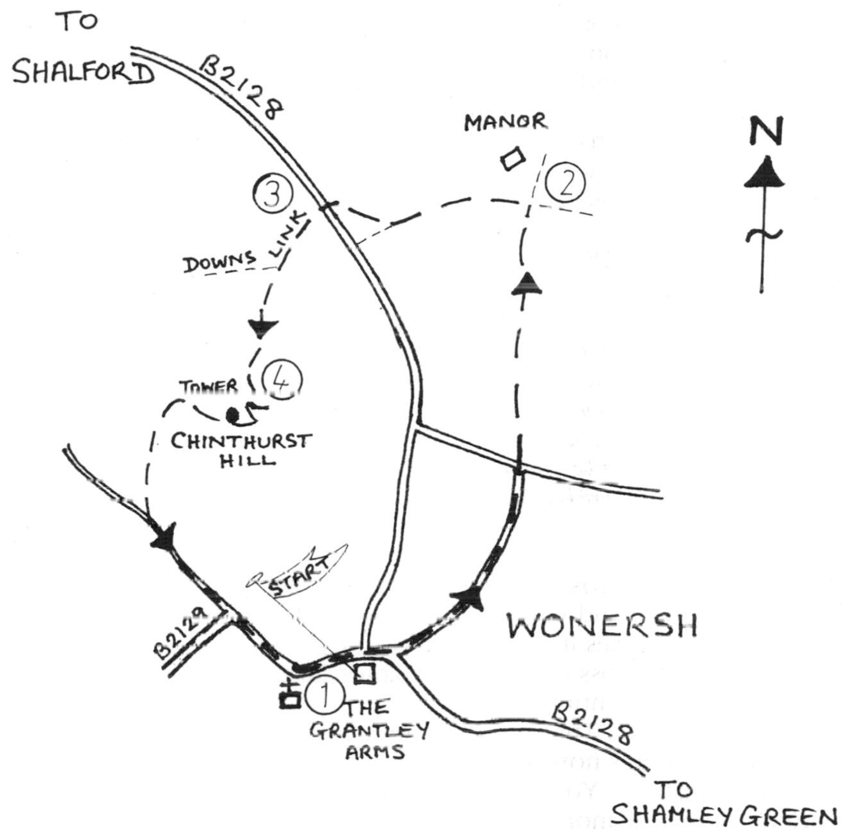

a large house over on your left. Go between two short posts onto a tarred driveway and turn right. Just before the driveway turns sharply left, cut the corner by taking a short path which leads you back onto it. Continue down the driveway and meet a road, where you turn left. You are led to another road where you cross over and turn left, passing some interesting old houses along the way. You may later prefer to cross back to take advantage of the pavement. Shortly you will find the church of St John the Baptist on the right. There is an interesting inscription on the gateway, which once led to Wonersh Park and now leads to the village green. Very shortly you are back at the pub.